HOUGHTON MIFFLIN SOCIAL STUDIES

From Sea to Shining Sea

O beautiful for spacious skies,

For amber waves of grain,

For purple mountain majesties

Above the fruited plain.

America! America! God shed His grace on thee,

And crown thy good with brotherhood

From sea to shining sea.

Katharine Lee Bates

Beverly J. Armento
Gary B. Nash
Christopher L. Salter
Karen K. Wixson

From Sea to Shining Sea

Houghton Mifflin Company • Boston

Atlanta • Dallas • Geneva, Illinois • Princeton, New Jersey • Palo Alto • Toronto

Consultants

Program Consultants

Edith M. Guyton
Associate Professor of Early
  Childhood Education
Georgia State University
Atlanta, Georgia

Gail Hobbs
Associate Professor of Geography
Pierce College
Woodland Hills, California

Charles Peters
Reading Consultant
Oakland Schools
Pontiac, Michigan

Cathy Riggs-Salter
Social Studies Consultant
Hartsburg, Missouri

Alfredo Schifini
Limited English Proficiency Consultant
Los Angeles, California

George Paul Schneider
Associate Director
  of General Programs
Department of Museum Education
Art Institute of Chicago
Chicago, Illinois

Twyla Stewart
Center for Academic Interinstitutional
  Programs
University of California—Los Angeles
Los Angeles, California

Scott Waugh
Associate Professor of History
University of California—Los Angeles
Los Angeles, California

Teacher Reviewers

David E. Beer (Grade 5)
Weisser Park Elementary
Fort Wayne, Indiana

Jan Coleman (Grades 6–7)
Thornton Junior High
Fremont, California

Shawn Edwards
  (Grades 1–3)
Jackson Park Elementary
University City, Missouri

Barbara J. Fech (Grade 6)
Martha Ruggles School
Chicago, Illinois

Deborah M. Finkel
  (Grade 4)
Los Angeles Unified
  School District,
  Region G
South Pasadena,
  California

Jim Fletcher (Grades 5, 8)
La Loma Junior High
Modesto, California

Susan M. Gilliam
  (Grade 1)
Roscoe Elementary
Los Angeles, California

Vicki Stroud Gonterman
  (Grade 2)
Gibbs International
  Studies Magnet School
Little Rock, Arkansas

Lorraine Hood (Grade 2)
Fresno Unified School
  District
Fresno, California

Jean Jamgochian
  (Grade 5)
Haycock Gifted and
  Talented Center
Fairfax County, Virginia

Susan Kirk-Davalt
  (Grade 5)
Crowfoot Elementary
Lebanon, Oregon

Mary Molyneaux-Leahy
  (Grade 3)
Bridgeport Elementary
Bridgeport, Pennsylvania

Sharon Oviatt
  (Grades 1–3)
Keysor Elementary
Kirkwood, Missouri

Jayne B. Perala (Grade 1)
Cave Spring Elementary
Roanoke, Virginia

Carol Siefkin (K)
Garfield Elementary
Sacramento, California

Norman N. Tanaka
  (Grade 3)
Martin Luther King Jr.
  Elementary
Sacramento, California

John Tyler (Grades 5, 8)
Groton School
Groton, Massachusetts

Portia W. Vaughn
  (Grades 1–3)
School District 11
Colorado Springs,
  Colorado

Acknowledgments

Grateful acknowledgment is made
for the use of the material listed below.
10–17 *Where the River Begins* by Thomas
Locker. Copyright © 1984 by Thomas
Locker. Reprinted by permission of
the publisher, Dial Books for Young
Readers.

–Continued on page 254.

From Your Authors

B lack Kettle licked buffalo grease from his lips and sighed happily. He looked at the other Cheyenne sitting around the campfire and knew they felt the same way. Their stomachs had not been full for a long time.

So begins the story of Black Kettle, a Cheyenne Indian boy about your age. In Chapter 5 of this book, you will have the chance to read more about Black Kettle and about those Indians who followed the buffalo.

Many of the people you will meet in this book lived long ago in places that may seem far away from your home. But they all had feelings just like yours. They had many of the same needs that you have today.

As you read about these people, places, and events, we hope you will ask many questions. Some questions may be about what things were like long ago. Other questions may be about the land. "What was it like in that place?" or "Why did those people choose to live there?" Still other questions may be about how they lived. "How did they get their food? or "What kind of houses did they live in?"

Most of all, we hope you continue to ask questions like these. We hope you enjoy asking questions and finding out answers, now and in the years to come.

Beverly J. Armento
Professor of Social Studies
Director, Center for Business and
Economic Education
Georgia State University

Christopher L. Salter
Professor and Chair
Department of Geography
University of Missouri

Gary B. Nash
Professor of History
University of California—Los Angeles

Karen K. Wixson
Associate Professor of Education
University of Michigan

Contents

Understanding Skills

Each "Understanding Skills" feature gives you the chance to learn and practice a skill.

Understanding Concepts

Each "Understanding Concepts" feature gives you information about an idea that is important to the lesson you have just read.

Making Decisions

Much of history is made up of people's decisions. Here you see how people make decisions. Then you practice how to make good decisions for yourself.

Explore

The story of the past is hidden in the world around you. "Explore" pages tell you the secrets of how to find it.

Literature

Reading these stories will help you experience what life was like at other times and places.

Primary Sources

Reading the exact words of people who lived long ago is a good way to learn about that time.

A Closer Look

Take a closer look at the objects and pictures on these pages. With the clues you see, you'll become a detective.

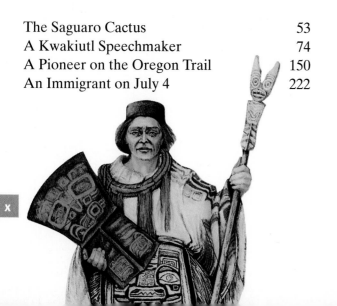

A Moment in Time

You can pretend to be there, at a moment in time. You'll get to know someone or something by the words and pictures on these pages.

How Much Does the World Recycle?

The United States recycles about 10% of its trash.

Western Europe recycles about 30%.

Japan recycles about 50%.

Wouldn't it be great if we could recycle all our trash?

Charts, Diagrams, and Timelines

These pictures help give you a clearer idea of the people, places, and events you are studying.

Maps

Often the land shapes the way things happen. Each map in this book tells a story about things that have happened and the places where they happened.

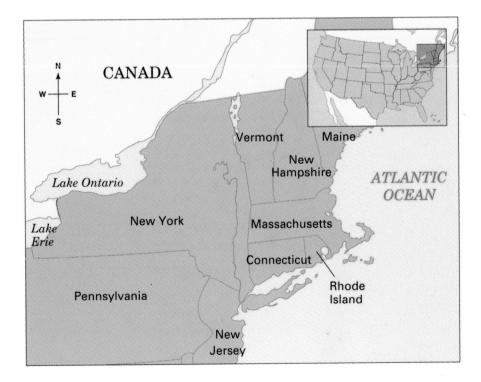

Starting Out

What makes this textbook so much more interesting than others you've used? Take some time, and look at each part of your book.

When and what? This number tells you which lesson you are reading. The title tells you what the lesson is about.

From unit to chapter to lesson— the art and photos show you where events happened.

Right from the beginning the lesson opener pulls you into the sights, the sounds, the smells of life at another time, in another place.

LESSON 2

Running Rivers

THINKING FOCUS

How do rivers affect the land?

Key Terms

* river
* lake
* flood

*T*he river went on raising and raising for ten or twelve days, till at last it was over the banks. The water was three or four foot deep on the island in the low places and on the Illinois bottom. On that side it was a good many miles wide, but on the Missouri side it was the same old distance across—a half a mile—because the Missouri shore was just a wall of high bluffs.

Daytimes we paddled all over the island in the canoe.... Well, on every old broken-down tree you could see rabbits and snakes and such things; and when the island had been overflowed a day or two they got so tame, on account of being hungry, that you could paddle right up and put your hand on them if you wanted to; but not the snakes and turtles—they would slide off in the water.

Mark Twain, from *The Adventures of Huckleberry Finn*

The author who wrote these words lived along a river bank and often saw the water rise after a big rain. A **river** is a stream of water that flows across land. Rivers are different from oceans in two ways. First, oceans are much bigger than rivers are. Oceans cover most of the earth. Second, oceans are salty. Rivers are not. Water that comes from rivers is called fresh water.

18

Like a road sign, the question that always appears here tells you what to think about while you read the lesson.

Look for these key terms. They are listed here so that you can watch for them. The first time they appear in the lesson they are shown in heavy black print and defined. Key terms are also defined in the Glossary.

Every age has its great storytellers. Each chapter includes short examples of fine writing from or about the period.

Take a closer look, in this case at the Grand Canyon. Look at the layers and layers of rock cut out by the river. Trace the route of the river on its way to Mexico.

A CLOSER LOOK
The Grand Canyon

The power of a river can change the earth. The Colorado River has formed a huge canyon by working its way through layers of rock. Every year, for millions of years, the canyon has become deeper and wider.

Millions of years ago, sand, gravel, and boulders were swept along by the river. These materials scraped away layers and layers of rock.

What was once a river bed is now the Grand Canyon. The Colorado River started out on flat land. Today it is a mile deep and almost 20 miles wide in some places.

John Wesley Powell, standing on the right, explored the Grand Canyon by boat, in 1869. Few people knew about the canyon's beauty until Powell shared information he learned on his journey.

The Route of the Colorado River

Utah
Nevada
Colorado River
Colorado
California
Grand Canyon National Park
Arizona
New Mexico
MEXICO

Trace the route of the Colorado River. It starts in Colorado and flows almost 1500 miles to Mexico. The gold area on this map shows Grand Canyon National Park. Each year, millions of people visit this park.

Fossils may be found where the Colorado River has cut down through layers of rock. Fossils are the remains or traces of past plants or animals. This fossil shows a fern that once grew in the canyon.

21

A **lake** is a pool of water on land. Like rivers, most lakes have fresh water. One difference between rivers and lakes is that rivers flow from place to place.

Constant Motion

Rivers start in different ways. Some rivers begin in lakes. Look at the map. Where does the Hudson River begin? Other rivers start from underground streams. Heavy rains or melting snow can also cause rivers. Rivers carry extra water that the land can't soak up.

The Hudson River

CANADA
Lake Ontario
Vermont
Maine
Lake Tear-of-the-Clouds
New Hampshire
ATLANTIC OCEAN
New York
Massachusetts
Lake Erie
Connecticut
Rhode Island
Pennsylvania
New Jersey

Once they begin, rivers are always moving. Most rivers run into another body of water. Some rivers flow into other rivers. Some rivers end in lakes or oceans. Others may just disappear underground.

Rivers may be wide or narrow. They may be deep or shallow. But all river water moves because it flows downhill. If the land is flat, water runs slowly. If the land is steep, water runs quickly. The Colorado River often flows fast because it runs downhill through very steep land. ■

▲ The Hudson River starts in Lake Tear-of-the-Clouds, which holds water from Mt. Marcy. Where does the river end?

■ How do rivers begin and end?

19

Pictured at a moment in time is this cactus in an Arizona desert. Look at its blossoms and the birds and rabbit that come to visit it. You will learn what happens to the cactus after a spring rain.

A MOMENT IN TIME
The Saguaro Cactus

10:32 A.M. May 5, 1991
After a spring rain in the Sonoran Desert in Arizona

Elf Owl
The unusual sound of falling rain woke this tiny owl from its daytime sleep. During the day, the owl hides in this hole made by a woodpecker months ago. At night, it leaves the nest to hunt.

Flowers
Raindrops sparkle on these blossoms that opened during the cool night hours. The flowers will close again before the afternoon heat reaches 110°F.

Arm
Sharp thorns cover the arms that show that this cactus is very old. A saguaro doesn't grow arms until it's at least 75 years old. Some saguaros live 250 years. They may stand 50 feet tall and have 50 arms.

Woodpecker
A loud tap, tap, tap fills the desert air as this bird pecks a hole in the trunk of the cactus. Today, it will find plenty of water inside. Later, another bird will build a nest in this hole.

Jack Rabbit
After nibbling tender young cactus sprouts in the early morning, this rabbit has hopped into the cool shade of the saguaro. There it can avoid the scorching sun until late afternoon.

Trunk
Swollen to twice its normal size, the trunk is filled with hundreds of gallons of rain water. The saguaro's roots quickly soaked up the water from the desert sands.

Every map tells a story. The map on this page tells the story of where the Hudson River in New York State runs and what the land is like there.

Continuing On

As you read about your world and the people in it, you'll want ways of understanding and remembering them better. This book gives you some tools to use in learning about people and places and remembering what you've learned.

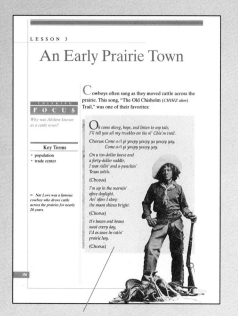

The titles give the main points of the lesson. On this page the red title tells you how rivers shape the land. On the next page the red title tells how rivers flood the land.

Shaping the Land

You saw how the mighty Colorado River carved a deep canyon into the surface of the earth. Other rivers cut valleys into the land, too. At first a river valley is narrow with steep sides, like the letter V. Over many years, the flow of water wears away the soil and rock of the banks and of the river bottom. In time, the V becomes deeper and wider.

Often the valley becomes very wide. The river may wander in winding loops from side to side. A river may change directions. This makes the valley even wider. If a river changes directions many times, it starts to look like many winding loops. Sometimes a river cuts off one of these loops, forming a C-shaped lake. ■

▼ *Look at the winding loops of this big, old river.*

■ *How do rivers change the shape of a valley?*

The Changing River

A loop in a river is called a meander.

In time, the river may flow out of its banks, straight ahead. The loop it leaves behind is called an ox-bow lake.

The people of the past speak directly to you in special parts of the text.

You're in charge of your reading. See the red square at the end of the text? Now find the red square over in the margin. If you can answer the question there, then you probably understood what you just read. If you can't, perhaps you'd better go back and read that part of the lesson again.

Diagrams make clear things that are hard to understand. Here the diagrams show the loops a river makes as it flows toward the sea.

Some tools you'll always use. The Understanding pages help you learn skills that you will use again and again. On this page you learn how to make a summary by listing the main ideas of what you've read.

You get the inside story when you read two special paragraphs. One, called How Do We Know?, tells you where information about the past comes from. Another, Across Time & Space, connects what you're reading to things that happpened long ago or far away. (See page 81 for an example.)

A picture is worth a thousand words. But just a few words in a caption can help you understand a picture, a map, or a photograph.

A special kind of Understanding page looks at the big ideas that help put all the pieces together. This section helps you understand ideas like how we use our natural resources—our water, land, and trees.

After you read the lesson, stop and review what you've read. The questions and an activity help you think about the lesson. Chapter Review questions help you tie the lessons together. (See pages 24 and 25 for an example.)

UNDERSTANDING A SUMMARY

Using Main Ideas

Here's Why Have you ever had to remember something you read? Maybe it was for a test. Or maybe you wanted to tell a friend. How do you go about remembering what you read? A good way to remember what you read is to make a summary of it.

Here's How A summary is a few sentences that tell the main ideas of what you read. You should use as few words as possible in a summary. They should be your own words.

In the last lesson, you read about Arbor Day. What would you include in a summary about Arbor Day? Think about the main ideas. The meaning of Arbor Day is one important idea to remember. When we celebrate Arbor Day is another. The number of years that Johnny Appleseed planted trees is a detail. Details are not as important as main ideas. They are not part of a summary.

Try It Work with a partner. Write a summary of the information about Arbor Day on pages 219 and 220.

Apply It Write a summary of something you have read in a book or magazine. Read your summary to the class.

---

the Land

...hat overflows its banks and covers land that is ...ry is a **flood.** Too much rain can cause a flood. ...ause might be the sudden melting of snow or ...hat is covered with water during a flood is ...ood plain.

...floods are harmful. They damage homes and ...soil. But some floods are helpful. Sometimes a ...ngs new soil and leaves it behind when the water ... The new soil helps crops grow better. Rivers may ...ay the land by erosion, but they can also build up ...d. ■

How Do We Know?

Much of Louisiana was built up by the Mississippi River. We know this because Louisiana's soil is made up of river sand, gravel, and mud. Since the Mississippi ends in Louisiana, it drops these materials before joining the Atlantic Ocean.

◁ This whole area is a flood plain. You can see that the farmer's house barely missed going underwater too. Farms are often on flood plains because the soil is so good.

■ How can a flood bring good things to people?

REVIEW

1. **FOCUS** How do rivers affect the land?
2. **CONNECT** What are the differences between oceans, rivers, and lakes?
3. **CRITICAL THINKING** We know that rivers drain water from the land. What do you think would happen if there were no rivers to carry off extra water?
4. **ACTIVITY** Take an imaginary trip on an ocean or a river. Write a short description of what you see, hear, and smell. Compare what you wrote with what your classmates wrote. How are river and ocean trips different? How are they the same?

UNDERSTANDING NATURAL RESOURCES

We Use Natural Resources

The Cheyenne used the buffalo to provide food, clothing, and shelter. The buffalo were a natural resource. A natural resource is anything found in nature that people can use.

Trees, soil, and water were also natural resources for the Cheyenne. The poles that dogs dragged behind them and that held up Cheyenne tipis came from trees. The Cheyenne raised crops in the soil and drank water from streams.

Today, we use many of the same natural resources. We use trees to make everything from houses to paper to clothing. We also use the soil to grow food. We drink water that comes from rivers, lakes, and underground wells.

Natural resources are also found inside the earth. Things like oil, coal, rocks, and metals are natural resources. Today, we use oil to make gasoline for cars. We burn coal in factories, and we use rocks to make cement sidewalks. We build many things, such as cars, with metals. These resources are as important to us as the buffalo were to the Cheyenne.

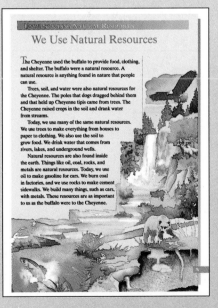

Also Featuring

Some special pages show up only once in every unit, not in every lesson in the book. These features continue the story by letting you explore an idea or activity, or read a story about another time and place. The Time/Space Databank in the back of the book brings together helpful pages you will use again and again.

What would you do? The Making Decisions pages show you an important decision. Then you practice the steps that will help you to make a good choice.

MAKING DECISIONS
Getting Farm Products to Stores

Here's How

Your crops can be shipped by truck, airplane, or train. You may have to use more than one method of transportation. Use the chart below to help you decide how to ship your crops.

EXPLORE
The Land Around You

What is the land like where you live? Are there rivers or lakes nearby? Is the land flat or is it hilly? Rivers, lakes, oceans, mountains, and hills are all physical features. You can explore the area where you live to find out more about its physical features.

Get Ready Begin by looking at the land near where you live. Then look at the land near your school and other places you visit close to home. Start a notebook of the physical features you see around you. Write about what you see. Draw pictures of the land you explore. You can also learn more about the land where you live by looking at maps and photographs.

Find Out Make a map of your area to show how the land looks. Use the notes and drawings in your notebook for help. You may also use photographs and maps from books and newspapers for help.

I see a river and a hill.

Move Ahead The map you made is on a flat piece of paper. All the physical features you drew on the map are flat. To show more exactly how the land looks, you can make a model from your map. Build your model with materials that you have at home or in your classroom. Clay and small rocks can be hills or mountains. Aluminum foil or plastic wrap can be rivers or lakes. Can you think of other materials to use?

Explore Some More Share your model with your classmates and other students in your school. Set up a display in your classroom. Label the models and show the maps you drew. Be ready to answer questions about your model and about the land in your area.

School isn't the only place where you can learn social studies. This feature gives you a chance to explore people and places outside the classroom—at home or in your own neighborhood.

Stories have always been important parts of people's lives. Each unit in the book has at least one story about the time and place you're studying. In this case, it's a story about a pioneer family in Kansas.

Many years ago, men, women, and children—young and old alike—went west to find a new land to settle. Travel was not easy. Houses and food were hard to find. But, always, other people helped. Read this excerpt from a story about a pioneer family in Kansas.

LITERATURE
WAGON WHEELS

Written by Barbara Brenner
Illustrated by Don Bolognese

Chapter 1—THE DUGOUT

There it is, boys," Daddy said. "Across this river is Nicodemus, Kansas. That is where we are going to build our house. There is free land for everyone here in the West. All we have to do is go and get it."

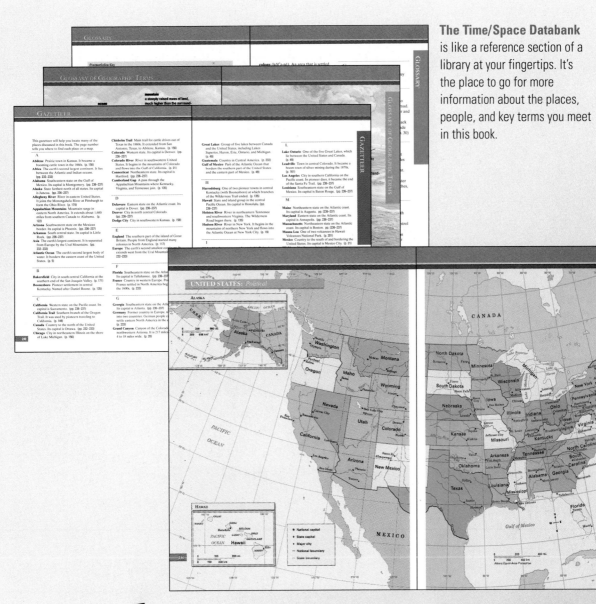

The Time/Space Databank is like a reference section of a library at your fingertips. It's the place to go for more information about the places, people, and key terms you meet in this book.

The Atlas maps out the world. Large maps show you the parts of your world and your country. One large map shows you the physical regions of the United States.

We had come a long way to get to Kansas. All the way from Kentucky. It had been a hard trip, and a sad one. Mama died on the way. Now there were just the four of us—Daddy, Willie, Little Brother, and me. "Come on, boys," Daddy called. "Let's put our feet on free dirt." We crossed the river, wagon and all.

Unit 1

Listen to the Land

Before people came to the land, only the sounds of nature could be heard. Water from melting snow rushed noisily down mountain peaks, and moose called in thick green forests. Today, roaring cars and planes can make them hard to hear, but—if you listen—you can still hear the beautiful sounds of the land.

David Muench. Beaver Lodge. Grand Teton National Park, Wyoming.

Chapter 1

Mighty Waters

The story of this land begins with a look at its mighty waters. The United States is touched by two great oceans and crossed by many rivers and streams. Pounding ocean waves eat away at the shores and make sandy beaches. Powerful rivers and streams carry soil from one place to another. The United States is a land shaped by water.

Oceans are filled with beautiful sea creatures. This animal is called a starfish, or a sea star. Starfish live in every ocean of the world.

Powerful waves have formed these cliffs along the Pacific Ocean.

The waters of the Atlantic Ocean broke up rocks and shells to form the sand on this beach.

The Earth is mostly covered with water. The United States lies between the Atlantic and Pacific oceans.

The Mississippi River, which winds through the middle of the United States, is the second longest river in North America. The Missouri River is the longest river in North America.

Sand and Salt

How do oceans change the land?

Key Terms

- ocean
- coast
- erosion

The sun was hot, but Matt didn't notice. He piled cool, damp sand onto his sand castle. The crashing waves of the ocean were so loud that he could barely hear the sea gulls calling. Matt picked up more sand and noticed something white, round, and flat. He carefully brushed off the sand. It was the first sand dollar Matt had ever found. He gently placed it next to the shells he had gathered.

Matt looked at the waves rolling toward him. He licked his lips, which tasted salty. Soon the waves would wash away his sand castle, but Matt didn't mind. He'd always have the sand dollar to remind him of the sea.

Pacific and Atlantic

The waves that rolled toward Matt came from the Pacific Ocean. An **ocean** is a large body of salt water. Oceans cover more than half the earth's surface. The Pacific Ocean is the largest ocean. It borders the United States on the west. Hawaii is surrounded by the Pacific Ocean.

If Matt could see 3,000 miles across the United States, he would see another ocean! That one is the Atlantic Ocean, the second largest ocean in the world. Find the Pacific and Atlantic oceans on the picture of the globe. ■

Coastal Land

Oceans constantly change the land. The land along the edge of an ocean is called the **coast.** Ocean waters act like a scraper on coastal land. Crashing waves slowly grind up the soil and rock and carry it away. This wearing away of land is called **erosion.**

Across Time & Space

Many scientists believe that the earth was once one giant piece of land and one giant ocean. Look at the world map on pages 232-233. Imagine that Africa and South America are pieces of a puzzle. Fit them together.

■ *What oceans border the United States?*

◄ *Large ocean waves like these can change the shape of a coast.*

Ocean waves are very powerful. Over hundreds of years, they can wear away even the hardest kinds of rock. In some places, crashing waves turn land along the coast into steep, rocky cliffs.

How Sea Cliffs Are Formed

1. A sea cliff starts out as a hill. Over many years, waves weaken the lower part of the hill.

2. Bit by bit, the earth and rock there begin to break into chunks and slide into the ocean.

3. Now the upper part of the hill hangs out over the water. When it becomes too heavy, that part begins to crumble and fall.

4. Finally, the side of the hill has become a steep cliff.

Ocean waves do not just cause erosion. They can also add to the land. When waves wash up on a shore, they may leave sand and mud behind. After years of sand and mud piling up this way, new beaches are formed.

Where does sand come from? You may be surprised to learn that it was once rocks and shells. Rocks and shells are pounded by waves against other rocks and shells. This constant pounding breaks them down into small bits. Then the waves wash the small bits onto the shore.

Not all beaches are alike. In some places, rocks and shells are broken into tiny bits and become sand. In other places, rocks do not break into such small pieces. That is why some beaches are sandy and others are rocky. ■

■ *How does the ocean take away land and give land back?*

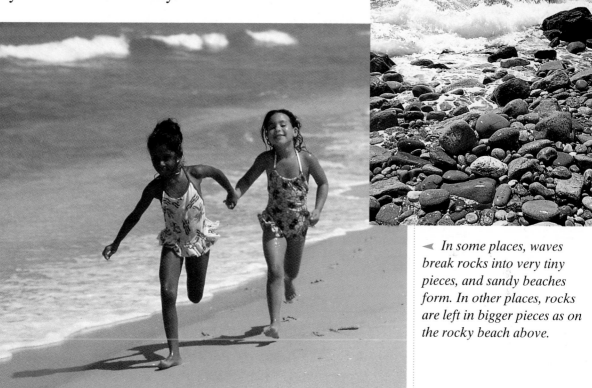

◄ *In some places, waves break rocks into very tiny pieces, and sandy beaches form. In other places, rocks are left in bigger pieces as on the rocky beach above.*

R E V I E W

1. **FOCUS** How do oceans change the land?
2. **CONNECT** Do you live closer to the Atlantic Ocean or the Pacific Ocean?
3. **CRITICAL THINKING** Is a sea cliff a safe place to build a house? Why?
4. **ACTIVITY** Draw a line down the middle of a piece of paper. On one side, draw a picture of things to do on a sandy beach. On the other side, draw a picture of things to do on a rocky beach.

Using a Compass Rose

Here's Why You know that the Pacific Ocean borders the United States on the west. The Atlantic Ocean is on the east. Canada is to the north. Mexico is to the south. North, south, east, and west are the main, or cardinal, directions.

Suppose you want to find a place between north and east, or between east and south. Then you need in-between directions. In-between directions are called intermediate directions. Knowing how to use intermediate directions will make it easier to locate places on a map.

Here's How You will find a compass rose on many maps. A compass rose shows directions. Find the compass rose on the treasure map on the next page. North is at the top. South is at the bottom. East is to the right. Where is west?

Now find the direction halfway between north and east on the compass rose. Northeast is the intermediate direction between north and east. What two letters are used for this direction? Find the direction halfway between south and east on the compass rose. That direction is labeled SE. What does SE stand for? What is the intermediate direction halfway between south and west? What is the intermediate direction halfway between north and west?

Try It Look at the treasure map again. Imagine that you are looking for hidden treasure. You walk north along the path and then turn east. You come to the hut, but the treasure isn't there. You decide to look under the table. In which direction is the table from the hut? Maybe the treasure is under the bridge. In which direction is the bridge from the table?

Apply It Now work with a partner. Plan your own treasure hunt. Use the map to decide where to hide your treasure. Give your partner a starting point and directions to find it. When your partner has found the treasure, it's your turn to search. Follow your partner's directions until you find the treasure.

Two boys watched the river and wondered where it began. They asked their grandfather, who had lived near the river all his life. Together, they set out to find the beginning of the river. Read about their trip.

LITERATURE

WHERE THE RIVER BEGINS

Written and Illustrated by Thomas Locker

Once there were two boys named Josh and Aaron who lived with their family in a big yellow house. Nearby was a river that flowed gently into the sea. On summer evenings the boys liked to sit on their porch watching the river and making up stories about it. Where, they wondered, did the river begin.

Their grandfather loved the river and had lived near it all his life. Perhaps he would know. One day Josh and Aaron asked their grandfather to take them on a camping trip to find the beginning of the river. When he agreed, they made plans and began to pack.

They started out early the next morning. For a time they walked along a familiar road past fields of golden wheat and sheep grazing in the sun. Nearby flowed the river—gentle, wide, and deep.

At last they reached the foothills of the mountains. The road had ended and now the river would be their only guide. It raced over rocks and boulders and had become so narrow that the boys and their grandfather could jump across.

In the late afternoon, while the sun was still hot, the river led them into a dark forest. They found a campsite and set up their tent. Then the boys went wading in the cold river water.

The first long day away from home was over.
That night, around the flickering campfire, their
grandfather told Josh and Aaron stories. Drifting
off to sleep, they listened to the forest noises and
were soothed by the sound of the river.

Dawn seemed to come quickly and the sun glowed through a thick mist. The boys were eager to be off, but their grandfather was stiff from sleeping on the ground and was slower getting started.

The path they chose led them high above the river. On a grassy knoll they stopped to gaze around. The morning mist had risen and formed white clouds in the sky. In the distance the river meandered lazily. It was so narrow that it seemed almost to disappear. They all felt a great excitement, for they knew they were nearing the end of their journey.

Without a word the boys began to run. They followed the river for an hour or more until it trickled into a still pond, high in an upland meadow. In this small, peaceful place the river began. Finally their search was over.

As they started back, the sky suddenly darkened. Thunder crashed around them and lightning lit the sky. They pitched their tent and crawled inside just before the storm broke. Rain pounded on the roof of their small tent all night long, but they were warm and dry inside.

In the morning long before dawn they were awakened by a roaring, rushing sound. The river had swelled with the storm and was flooding its banks. They tried to take a shortcut across a field but were soon ankle deep in water. Grandfather explained that the river drew its waters from the rains high up in the mountains.

They came down out of the foothills in the soft light of late afternoon. The boys recognized the cliffs along the river and knew they were close to home. Their weariness lifted and they began to move more quickly down the road.

At last they reached their house on the hill. The boys raced ahead to tell their mother and father about the place where the river began. But their grandfather paused for a moment and in the fading light he watched the river, which continued on as it always had, flowing gently into the sea.

Running Rivers

THINKING FOCUS

How do rivers affect the land?

Key Terms

- river
- lake
- flood

*T*he river went on raising and raising for ten or twelve days, till at last it was over the banks. The water was three or four foot deep on the island in the low places and on the Illinois bottom. On that side it was a good many miles wide, but on the Missouri side it was the same old distance across—a half a mile—because the Missouri shore was just a wall of high bluffs.

Daytimes we paddled all over the island in the canoe. . . . Well, on every old broken-down tree you could see rabbits and snakes and such things; and when the island had been overflowed a day or two they got so tame, on account of being hungry, that you could paddle right up and put your hand on them if you wanted to; but not the snakes and turtles—they would slide off in the water.

Mark Twain, from *The Adventures of Huckleberry Finn*

The author who wrote these words lived along a river bank and often saw the water rise after a big rain. A **river** is a stream of water that flows across land. Rivers are different from oceans in two ways. First, oceans are much bigger than rivers are. Oceans cover most of the earth. Second, oceans are salty. Rivers are not. Water that comes from rivers is called fresh water.

A **lake** is a pool of water on land. Like rivers, most lakes have fresh water. One difference between rivers and lakes is that rivers flow from place to place.

Constant Motion

Rivers start in different ways. Some rivers begin in lakes. Look at the map. Where does the Hudson River begin? Other rivers start from underground streams. Heavy rains or melting snow can also cause rivers. Rivers carry extra water that the land can't soak up.

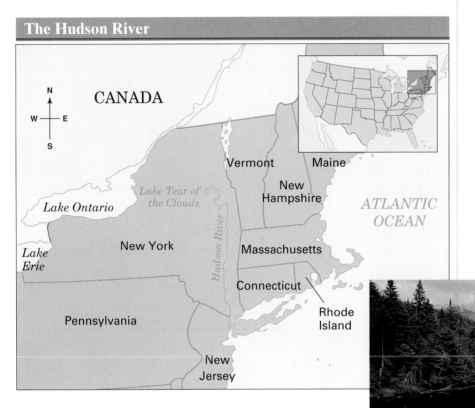

The Hudson River

CANADA

N
W — E
S

Vermont   Maine

New
Hampshire

Lake Ontario

Lake Tear of the Clouds

ATLANTIC
OCEAN

New York   Massachusetts

Hudson River

Lake
Erie

Connecticut

Rhode
Island

Pennsylvania

New
Jersey

Once they begin, rivers are always moving. Most rivers run into another body of water. Some rivers flow into other rivers. Some rivers end in lakes or oceans. Others may just disappear underground.

Rivers may be wide or narrow. They may be deep or shallow. But all river water moves because it flows downhill. If the land is flat, water runs slowly. If the land is steep, water runs quickly. The Colorado River often flows fast because it runs downhill through very steep land. ■

The Hudson River starts in Lake Tear-of-the-Clouds, which holds water from Mt. Marcy. Where does the river end?

■ *How do rivers begin and end?*

19

The Grand Canyon

The power of a river can change the earth. The Colorado River has formed a huge canyon by working its way through layers of rock. Every year, for millions of years, the canyon has become deeper and wider.

Millions of years ago, sand, gravel, and boulders were swept along by the river. These materials scraped away layers and layers of rock.

What was once a river bed is now the Grand Canyon. The Colorado River started out on flat land. Today it is a mile deep and almost 20 miles wide in some places.

John Wesley Powell, standing on the right, explored the Grand Canyon by boat, in 1869. Few people knew about the canyon's beauty until Powell shared information he learned on his journey.

The Route of the Colorado River

Utah

Colorado River

Colorado

Nevada

Grand Canyon National Park

California

Arizona

New Mexico

MEXICO

Trace the route of the Colorado River. It starts in Colorado and flows almost 1500 miles to Mexico. The gold area on this map shows Grand Canyon National Park. Each year, millions of people visit this park.

Fossils may be found where the Colorado River has cut down through layers of rock. Fossils are the remains or traces of past plants or animals. This fossil shows a fern that once grew in the canyon.

Shaping the Land

You saw how the mighty Colorado River carved a deep canyon into the surface of the earth. Other rivers cut valleys into the land, too. At first a river valley is narrow with steep sides, like the letter V. Over many years, the flow of water wears away the soil and rock of the banks and of the river bottom. In time, the V becomes deeper and wider.

Often the valley becomes very wide. The river may wander in winding loops from side to side. A river may change directions. This makes the valley even wider. If a river changes directions many times, it starts to look like many winding loops. Sometimes a river cuts off one of these loops, forming a C-shaped lake. ■

▼ *Look at the winding loops of this big, old river.*

■ *How do rivers change the shape of a valley?*

The Changing River

A loop in a river is called a meander.

In time, the river may flow out of its banks, straight ahead. The loop it leaves behind is called an ox-bow lake.

Flooding the Land

Water that overflows its banks and covers land that is normally dry is a **flood.** Too much rain can cause a flood. Another cause might be the sudden melting of snow or ice. Land that is covered with water during a flood is called a flood plain.

Most floods are harmful. They damage homes and carry off soil. But some floods are helpful. Sometimes a flood brings new soil and leaves it behind when the water dries up. The new soil helps crops grow better. Rivers may take away the land by erosion, but they can also build up the land. ■

How Do We Know?

Much of Louisiana was built up by the Mississippi River. We know this because Louisiana's soil is made up of river sand, gravel, and mud. Since the Mississippi ends in Louisiana, it drops these materials before joining the Atlantic Ocean.

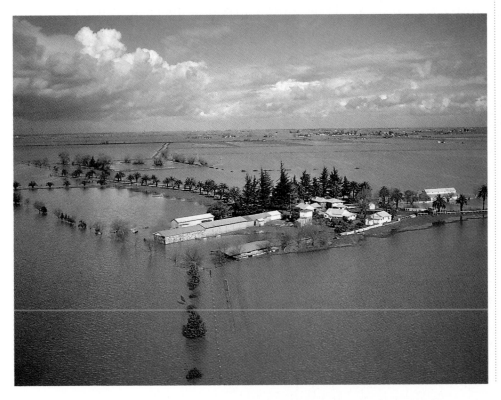

◄ *This whole area is a flood plain. You can see that the farmer's house barely missed going underwater too. Farms are often on flood plains because the soil is so good.*

■ *How can a flood bring good things to people?*

R E V I E W

1. **FOCUS** How do rivers affect the land?
2. **CONNECT** What are the differences between oceans, rivers, and lakes?
3. **CRITICAL THINKING** We know that rivers drain water from the land. What do you think would happen if there were no rivers to carry off extra water?
4. **ACTIVITY** Take an imaginary trip on an ocean or a river. Write a short description of what you see, hear, and smell. Compare what you wrote with what your classmates wrote. How are river and ocean trips different? How are they the same?

Chapter Review

Reviewing Key Terms

coast (p. 5)   lake (p. 19)
erosion (p. 5)   ocean (p. 5)
flood (p. 23)   river (p. 18)

A. Write the key term for each meaning.

1. a pool of water on land
2. the wearing away of land
3. a large body of salt water
4. the land that is along the edge of an ocean

B. Write the correct key term for each numbered blank.

On his vacation, Jack saw big waves of salt water in the __1__. His mother told him that the waves caused __2__ of the land. Amy went to a __3__, which is a large pool of fresh water. From it, a __4__ began and flowed downhill between its banks. One day, too much rain caused a __5__.

Exploring Concepts

A. Copy the chart below. Fill in the missing information in the two empty spaces. In the second column, fill in the kind of water that rivers have. In the last column, fill in the size of oceans. Your chart will show two ways in which rivers and oceans are different.

B. Write one or two sentences to answer each question.

1. How are floods helpful and how are they harmful?
2. How are some new beaches formed?
3. Explain why some river water runs slowly and some runs quickly.

Bodies of water	Kinds of water	Size
Rivers		Smaller than oceans
Oceans	Salty	

Reviewing Skills

1. Find Denver, Colorado, on the map on pages 234–235. Travel northwest from Denver to Canada. When you get near Canada, in what state will you be?
2. In what intermediate direction would you travel to go from Atlanta, Georgia, to the coast of Maine?
3. What state is next to and east of Mississippi? What two states are next to Mississippi on the west?

Using Critical Thinking

1. You know that rivers change the land. How do you think the Colorado River will continue to change the Grand Canyon?
2. Suppose you take a boat trip down a long river. You go all the way to the end of the river. What might you see there?

Preparing for Citizenship

1. **ART ACTIVITY** Look at the river pictures on the right. Then read Mark Twain's description of the river on page 18 again. Draw a picture that shows the scene described by Mark Twain. Color your picture if you want to.
2. **COLLABORATIVE LEARNING** Work with a partner. Have one person be a newspaper reporter who asks the other person questions about the effects of a flood on the land. Then switch roles so that the reporter becomes the person who answers questions. Finally, work together to write a newspaper story about the effects of the flood. Be sure to include some of the interview answers. If you can, read your story to your class.

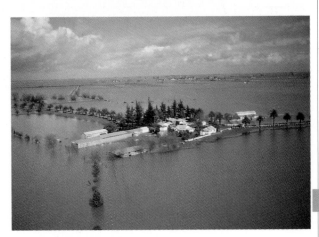

Chapter 2

Rustling Leaves and Grasses

Our mighty rivers flow across a huge land. Not all of this land looks the same. The rivers flow through great tree-covered lands called forests. They also cross huge grasslands called prairies. Forests and prairies are very different from each other, but they are both home to many kinds of animals.

A sage grouse can hide from its enemies in the tall grasses of a prairie.

This is turkeyfoot prairie grass. The tops of the grass separate into many parts and look like turkeys' feet.

Forests grow in much of the eastern half of the country. Forests also grow in many mountains and along the coasts in the West. Prairies cover much of the middle part of our land.

Many of the trees in this forest are oaks and maples. Sugar maple trees grow from seeds like the ones at the top of this page.

The color of this gray fox's fur makes it hard to see against the greens and browns of the forest. This helps it sneak up on the animals that are its food.

Wonderful Woodlands

Why are forests important?

Key Terms

- forest
- humus

Imagine being able to swing, hop, or fly from tree to tree all the way from the Atlantic Ocean to the Mississippi River without ever touching the ground! Long ago, the trees were so thick that a squirrel could have done just that. Most of the eastern half of our country was one big **forest,** a large area of land thickly covered with trees.

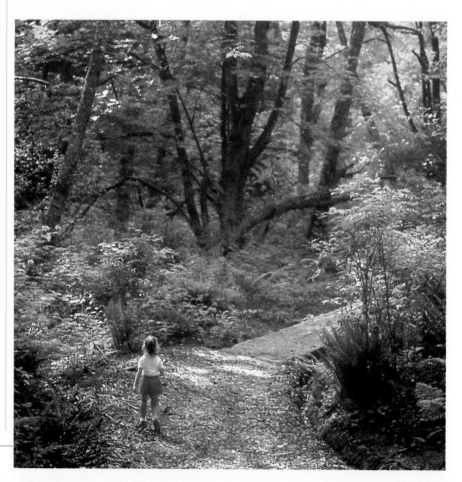

United States Forests

Today, trees no longer cover so much area. About 100 years ago, most of those forests were gone. As our country grew, people cut down trees to make room for farmland and cities. Today, people plant new forests to help replace some of those that once covered much of America.

Three types of forests grow in the United States. One kind has trees that lose their leaves in the fall. Another type of forest has trees that stay green all year. The third kind is a mixed forest. It includes trees that stay green and trees that lose their leaves. What kinds of trees grow where you live? ■

■ *What types of forests grow in the United States?*

Types of United States Forests

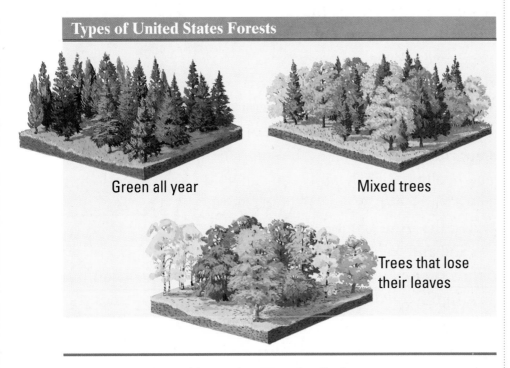

Green all year

Mixed trees

Trees that lose their leaves

◄ *Here are three types of forests in the fall. The trees that always stay green are called evergreens. The forest on the right is a mixed forest. Trees that lose their leaves have bare branches in the winter.*

Trees and Soil Help Each Other

Trees are important because they help stop erosion. You have already seen how water in oceans and rivers wear away the land. Wind can cause erosion, too.

Trees help stop erosion in two ways. First, their roots hold the soil in place. The roots act like tiny fingers. When the wind blows, the "fingers" grab on to the soil and keep the wind from taking it away. Trees also stop erosion by "feeding" the land. When a tree dies, its branches, roots,

How Do We Know?

Some trees can grow to be thousands of years old. Look at a round tree stump sometime. You can tell how old the tree was by counting the number of rings on the trunk. Each ring stands for one year.

➤ *The green moss on this dead log makes a good place for mushrooms and insects to live.*

▲ *Mushrooms get their food from dead plants. Mushrooms help break down dead trees into humus for rich new soil.*

■ *How do trees help the land?*

and leaves decay, or rot away. This decayed material is called **humus** *(HYOO muhs)*. The dark brown color of soil comes from humus. More important, humus makes the soil rich and healthy. Rich, healthy soil can hold more water. When the soil holds more water, the wind cannot easily blow it away.

Soil and water feed trees and other plants. When the soil is well-fed, trees and plants can be healthy, too. In other words, trees help soil and soil helps trees. ■

Trees and Animals Need Each Other

Soil and trees are not the only things that depend on each other. Forest plants and animals need each other, too. The forest gives food and shelter to many animals. Squirrels and birds make their homes in tree branches. Raccoons live in holes in tree trunks. Insects live in tree bark. Many animals eat the seeds and nuts that grow on trees. Deer eat bark. Insects eat leaves, wood, and roots.

In return, the animals help more trees and plants

◄ Birds and squirrels help forests grow. By eating berries, this thrush scatters seeds on the ground from which new plants sprout. By burying an acorn, and then forgetting to dig it up later for lunch, this squirrel helps plant new oak trees.

to grow. How? Trees and plants grow from seeds and nuts. Birds scatter seeds that allow new plants to grow. Have you ever seen a squirrel bury an acorn? Squirrels bury more nuts than they can eat. Each nut they bury has a chance to become a new tree.

Animals help the trees in another way. When they die, their bodies decay on the ground. The decaying bodies add to the humus in the soil that feeds the trees. The forest feeds its creatures, and the animals die and become food for the trees. In this way, forest life can go on and on.

So forest animals and plants depend on each other in many ways. If one living thing is damaged or destroyed, another may suffer, too. If whole forests are cut down, animals may lose their homes and die. Soil washes away and new plants cannot grow. If we learn how living things depend on each other, we can help forest life continue. ∎

■ *How do trees and animals help each other?*

R E V I E W

1. **FOCUS** Why are forests important?
2. **CONNECT** Would you rather visit a river or a forest? Why?
3. **CRITICAL THINKING** How might a forest be different if no animals lived in it?

4. **ACTIVITY** Draw a picture of a forest. In your picture, show how trees give shelter and food to animals.

Finding Supporting Details

Here's Why   Writers often write about one main idea in each paragraph. Other sentences give details that support, or explain, the main idea. Knowing how to find main ideas and their supporting details will help you understand what you read.

Here's How   Think of a chart such as the one below when you read a paragraph. The large box at the top has the main idea. The smaller boxes have the details. Read this paragraph:

> The forest is home to many animals. Birds make their nests in tree branches. Hollowed-out tree stumps are homes for raccoons and other animals. Deer sleep and hide among the trees in forests.

The main idea of the paragraph is: *The forest is home to many animals.* The other sentences tell how the forest is home to the animals. They give the details that support the main idea.

Main Idea: **The forest is home to many animals.**

Detail: Birds make their nests in tree branches.	**Detail:** Hollowed-out tree stumps are homes for raccoons and other animals.	**Detail:** Deer sleep and hide among the trees in forests.

Try It   Read the second paragraph on page 29 again. The main idea is stated in the first sentence. What details support the main idea?

Apply It   Work with a partner. Write a paragraph about forests or forest animals. Make a chart of your main idea and supporting details.

A Sea of Grass

Picture yourself standing in a field of grass. The grass is moving in the wind, like waves on the ocean. The land stretches out as far as you can see. Suddenly, the ground begins to shake. The land ahead looks dark and smoky. You begin to think the whole earth might be on fire! A rumbling sound grows louder and louder. Now you know that you are not looking at the smoke of a raging fire. What you see is the darkness of thousands of pawing and charging buffaloes coming toward you. A great cloud of dust blackens the sky for miles around.

THINKING FOCUS

How are prairies different from forests?

Key Terms

- prairie
- predator

◄ A Herd of Buffaloes on the Bed of the Missouri River *was painted by William Jacob Hays in 1860.*

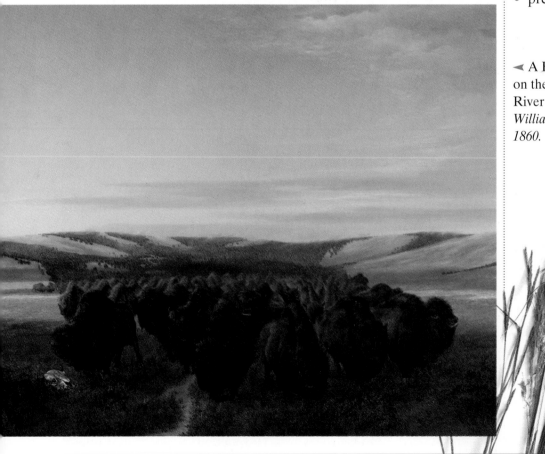

What Is a Prairie?

Across Time & Space

Two hundred years ago, millions of buffaloes roamed the U.S. prairies. Later, hunters killed all but about 500. Now buffaloes live in areas that are protected from hunters.

■ What would you see if you were standing on a prairie?

▼ This prairie in Nebraska grows short grass about two feet tall.

People traveling across the United States long ago would often write about seeing these giant animals. During the fall, small groups, or herds, of buffaloes joined together to form larger herds. In the winter, these huge herds would move across the prairie to warmer areas. There they searched for food. A **prairie** is an area of flat or hilly land covered by grasses.

If you stood in the middle of a great prairie, you would see nothing but grass and sky. In the distance, you might notice a low hill. You would not see many trees.

The amount of rain that falls on prairies affects the height of the grass that can grow there. Eastern prairies get more rain than western prairies. Because of this, grass in the east can grow as tall as a person!

Prairie soil is very rich. Grasses and farm crops, such as wheat and oats, grow well in such soil. Because of this, much of the prairie land shown on the map on page 35 is now used for raising animals and crops. ■

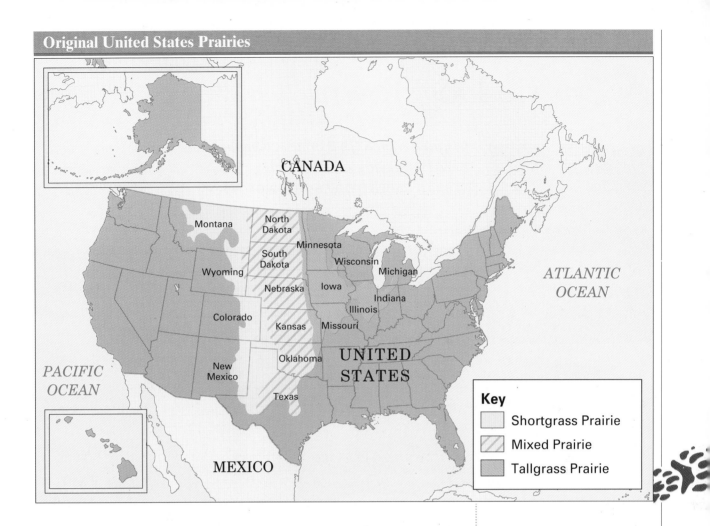

CANADA

Montana

North Dakota

Minnesota

South Dakota

Wisconsin

Michigan

Wyoming

Nebraska

Iowa

ATLANTIC OCEAN

Indiana

Illinois

Colorado

Kansas

Missouri

PACIFIC OCEAN

New Mexico

Oklahoma

UNITED STATES

Texas

MEXICO

Key

Shortgrass Prairie

Mixed Prairie

Tallgrass Prairie

Prairie Life

Prairies are home to many creatures. The animals that live on prairies have special ways to protect themselves from predators. A **predator** is an animal that hunts other animals for food. Forest animals use the trees to hide from their enemies. Since few trees grow on prairies, the animals there have other ways to escape predators.

Some prairie animals, such as badgers and prairie dogs, dig underground tunnels, or burrows, to protect themselves from predators. If an enemy is near and there is no burrow around, a badger will quickly dig a new one to hide in. Prairie dogs nibble down the grass around their burrows. Doing so makes it easier for prairie dogs to see predators coming.

◄ *Badgers have large front paws with sharp claws. How does this help them in their prairie life?*

35

A Prairie Dog Town

If you were to visit a prairie, what animals do you think you'd see? Prairie dogs live on prairies in large groups called towns. A town may have 50 to 100 burrows.

Prairie grass for lunch? Sounds delicious! Prairie dogs eat mostly grasses and grain. They also eat small insects.

Home means being together! Many prairie dogs live in one burrow. The entrance is called a mound.

Let's take a tour of a prairie dog burrow:
a. *emergency exit*—used to escape predators
b. *nursery or bedroom*—used to sleep or give birth
c. *bathroom*—used only during bad weather
d. *listening room*—used to listen for predators
e. *dry room*—used during floods

◄ The pronghorn's long legs help make it one of the fastest animals in the world.

▼ The coyote can leap 14 feet. How does this help make it a good predator?

Pronghorns protect themselves from predators by living in herds. When a predator is near, the animals warn each other. The animals in a herd also stay together. It is much harder for an enemy to attack a whole herd than to attack a single animal. If an animal gets separated from the herd, its best chance to escape is to outrun its enemy. Being able to run fast helps many animals stay alive on the prairie.

Who are these enemies? Coyotes *(ky OH teez)* are among the most feared predators. Coyotes hunt everything from the smallest prairie dog to the largest pronghorn. They are also very fast. Coyotes can outrun many small animals and are very good hunters. They have to be. After all, coyotes must stay alive in the sea of grass, too. ■

■ How do prairie animals protect themselves from predators?

R E V I E W

1. **FOCUS** How are prairies different from forests?
2. **CONNECT** Compare the way forest and prairie animals escape from predators.
3. **CRITICAL THINKING** Tell how living in a burrow in a prairie dog town is like living in an apartment in a big apartment building. How is it different?
4. **ACTIVITY** Imagine you are a traveler long ago, seeing a prairie and its animals for the first time. Write a paragraph in your journal telling what you see.

Line Graphs and Circle Graphs

Here's Why   Have you ever heard the expression "a picture is worth a thousand words"? Line graphs are like pictures of number facts. Knowing how to read line graphs will help you see changes over a period of time.

Circle graphs compare the amount of things. Knowing how to read circle graphs will help you understand differences in amounts.

Here's How   As you know, line graphs deal with numbers. The dots on a line graph represent numbers. We use line graphs to see how something changes. Look at the line graph below. It shows the amount of rain that fell on a prairie for six months during one year.

The numbers down the left side of the line graph are inches of rain. For April, the dot is at three inches of rainfall. The dot for May is at a larger number. The June

Prairie Rainfall for Six Months

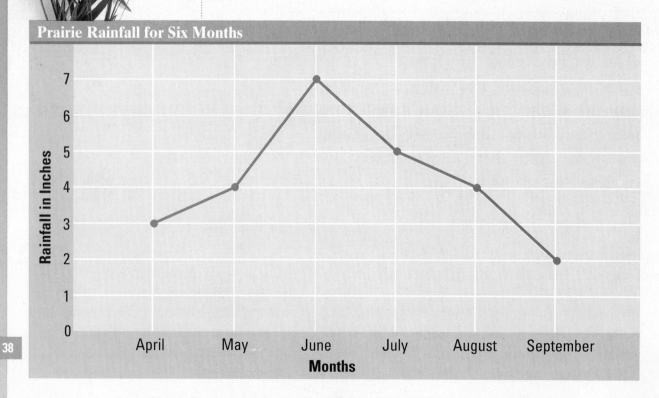

38

dot is at a still larger number. The dots are connected by lines to show the amount of change in rainfall during the six months. Which month had the most rainfall? Which had the least?

Circle graphs show parts of a whole. You have learned that different kinds of forests grow in the Northeast. The circle graph on this page shows how much of the Northeast is covered by each kind of forest. The key above the graph shows what the colors in the graph stand for. What color stands for mixed trees? You can see that most of the forest area is mixed trees, because that is the largest part of the circle.

Types of Northeast Forest

Mixed trees

Trees that lose their leaves

Trees that stay green all year

Try It   Look at the line graph again. How can you find the amount of rain that fell in July? How much rain fell in September? How much more rain fell in June than in September?

Now look at the circle graph again. What type of forest is shown by the smallest part of the graph? What does the graph tell you about the trees in that type of forest?

Apply It   Look in books, magazines, or newspapers for graphs. Find one line graph and one circle graph. Tell how your graphs show change in amounts or compare amounts.

Chapter 3

Majestic Peaks and Deserts

Much of the land in the western United States is made up of towering mountains or dry deserts. Mountaintops can be very cold, and deserts are often very hot. The animals and plants that live on these kinds of land must have special ways of staying alive.

Cactus plants have spines that protect them from animals that live in the desert. Without their spines, these plants would be eaten for the water inside.

This brightly colored lizard is a Gila *(HEE luh)* Monster. It is right at home in the blazing summer heat of an Arizona desert.

Bighorn sheep move easily over jagged rocks in high mountains.

This is one of the Sawtooth Mountains in Idaho. Few plants grow at the top of this high peak, but below you can see evergreen forests.

Touching the Clouds

How do mountains affect the land around them?

Key Terms

- mountain
- physical feature
- temperature
- timberline

➤ *These are the beautiful Teton (TEE tahn) Mountains in northwestern Wyoming. Find the highest peak. It is called Grand Teton.*

Ann stood on the edge of a cliff and caught her breath. She had been mountain climbing for years, but this sport was new to her. She was almost ready to go. She thought about her teacher's directions.

One end of her rope was firmly attached to the mountain. Ann had hooked the rope to her body, and now she gripped it with both hands. She backed slowly over the edge of the cliff and pushed off into space!

Down, down, down she went. The wind whistled past her ears. Her hands fed out more and more rope. Her feet touched the cliff face again and again. Ann was rappelling *(ra PEHL ihng)* down a mountain for the first time, and she loved it!

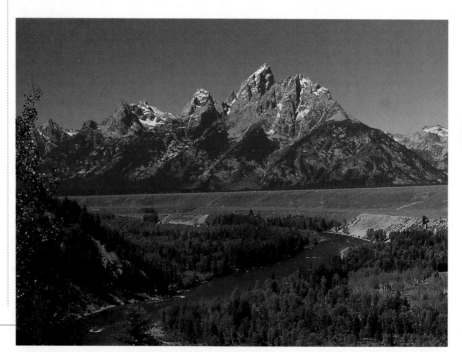

Height Makes a Difference

Mountain climbing, like rappelling, has many exciting moments. Climbing to the peak of a mountain is also hard work. And it's no wonder. A **mountain** is a piece of land that is higher than a hill and stands much higher than the land around it. This **physical feature,** or natural part of the earth's surface, is easy to see. A mountain has steep sides and a pointed or rounded top.

Air is cooler in high places than it is in low places. At the top of tall mountains, the temperature is very cold. The **temperature** of air is how hot or cold it is.

What does this colder air mean to plant life on mountains? Few plants are able to grow in the highest parts of tall mountains. The plants that do live there must be strong, indeed. They must be able to grow in very cold air and wind.

Different kinds of plants grow well at different heights. Oak and aspen trees grow well on the lower parts of a mountain. Only the very toughest trees, such as bristlecone pines, can grow at higher levels. No trees are able to grow at the highest levels. The height where trees can no longer grow is called the **timberline.** A few small plants can live above the timberline. Columbines and moss campions are wildflowers that can grow in this bitter cold.

▼ *The chart below shows two kinds of small flowers and two kinds of large trees that can grow at different heights on a mountain. When a person is standing far from a mountain, the wildflowers are too small to be seen.*

Plant Life on a Mountain

Timberline

Columbine

Moss Campion

Bristlecone Pine

Aspen

Because of the low temperatures, very few animals live above the timberline. Some animals, such as bighorn sheep, live there during late spring and summer. When fall comes, these wild sheep go down the mountain to avoid deep snow that will cover the grasses they feed on.

Bighorns have very little trouble traveling up and down the mountains. They are able to jump and climb quickly, even in very steep places. For this reason, bighorns can easily escape predators on rocky mountainsides. ■

➤ *"Bighorn" is a good name for these animals. Some bighorns have horns that are over four feet long.*

■ *How does height affect the plant and animal life on a mountain?*

Across Time & Space

Standing in the Rocky Mountains today, you'd never guess that this land was once under an ocean. Fossils of sea creatures are found in rocks all over these mountains.

46

A Powerful Force

Mountains affect more than just the plants and animals that live on them. Mountains are a powerful force that can change the weather a long distance away.

In the United States, clouds usually move from west to east. They must rise to pass over mountains. Remember that air gets colder at higher levels. Cold air cannot hold as much water as warm air can. As clouds begin to rise, the damp air grows cooler, so the clouds cannot hold as much water. The water falls in the form of rain or snow.

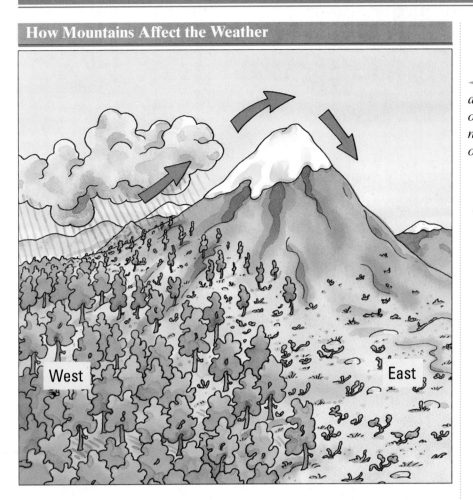

◄ How do you think the different amounts of rainfall on the east and west sides of a mountain affect the plant life on each side?

West

East

As the clouds drift over mountains, they may drop more water. By the time the clouds have moved farther east, most of their water is gone. This means more rain falls on land west of mountains and less rain falls on land east of them.

In the same way, mountains usually protect land to the east of them from high winds and snowstorms. These storms move from west to east, just as rain clouds do. The west sides of mountains get most of the storms, while the land east of the mountains is protected. ■

■ How does a mountain affect the weather in the area around it?

R E V I E W

1. **FOCUS** How do mountains affect the land around them?
2. **CONNECT** How does melting mountain snow affect some rivers?
3. **CRITICAL THINKING** How is plant and animal life on the highest parts of mountains different in the summer than it is in the winter?
4. **WRITING ACTIVITY** Decide whether you would rather live on the east side or the west side of a mountain. Write a paragraph telling why.

Reading a Physical Map

Here's Why   You know that mountains are one of the physical features of the earth's surface. Mountains and other physical features of an area can be shown on a physical map. There are many kinds of physical maps. One kind shows lowlands, highlands, and mountains. Lowlands are large areas of land that are at about the same level as the sea, or ocean. Highlands are high above sea level. Physical maps also show water features, such as oceans, lakes, and rivers.

Land Above Sea Level

Highlands

Lowlands

Sea Level

Here's How   Most physical maps use different colors to stand for different things. Blue usually stands for water. Green usually stands for lowlands. Every map has a map key that shows what the colors on the map stand for.

Look at the map key for the physical map on page 49. Notice the colors and what they stand for. What does yellow stand for? What does brown stand for?

Now look at the map itself. Find Lake Ontario. How does the map show that Lake Ontario is a body of water? Two rivers are also shown on the map. Trace the route of the Mississippi River with your finger. It begins in a northern state and ends at the Gulf of Mexico.

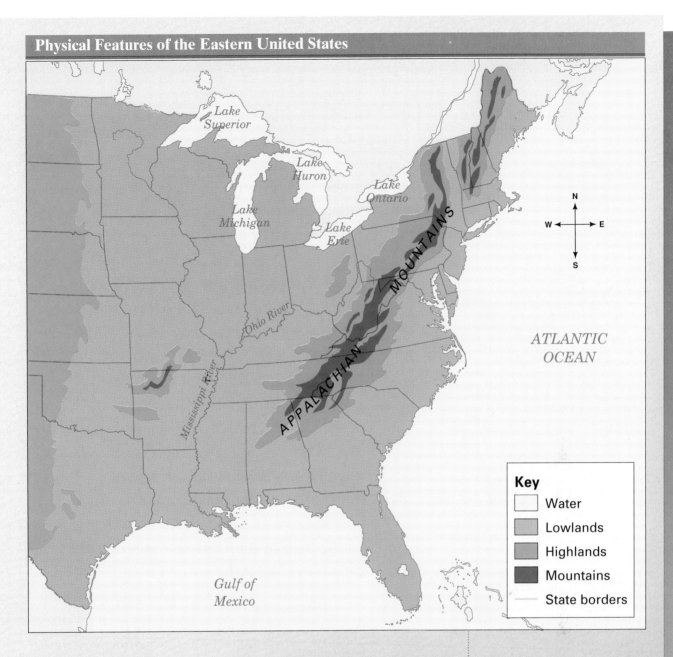

The map shows a long range of mountains through the eastern states of our country. Can you name any of these mountain states?

Try It   Work with a partner. Ask each other questions about the physical map on this page. For example, what is the largest lake shown on the map?

Apply It   Look at the physical map of the United States in the Atlas on pages 238–239. How are mountains shown on the map? Name two rivers that flow into the Mississippi River. What physical features are in or near the state of Alaska?

Physical Features and People

You have learned that physical features are the natural parts of the surface of the earth. A physical feature may be part of the earth's land or water. For example, a mountain is a land feature and an ocean is a water feature. A town is not a physical feature because it is not a natural part of the earth. A town is made by people. A drawing of many physical features is shown on pages 244–245 of the Time/Space Databank.

The earth's physical features have a lot to do with where people live and how people live. Many cities, for example, grew next to a river. Rivers have always provided transportation for people and the things people grow or make. Find some river cities on the map of the United States on pages 236–237 of the Atlas.

St. Louis, Missouri

Cities have also grown on ocean coasts. These cities often started near a harbor, which is an area of the ocean that is partly surrounded by land. The harbor provides a safe place for ships. Find some ocean cities on the map of the United States on pages 236–237.

There are many ways that physical features affect our lives. We do different things on a mountain than we do in a

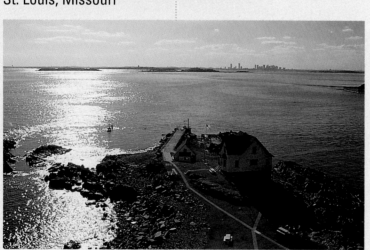

Boston, Massachusetts

lowland. We may even eat different foods. As you study about our country, you will learn more about the effects of physical features on the lives of people.

A Dry Place

Katie pressed her nose against the glass. Inside the clear case, the creature stared back. Its body was covered with tiny scales and it had a long, thin tail.

"Wow!" said Katie. "Look at that funny-looking animal. Maybe it's from another planet."

"Now, Katie," Mrs. King said, smiling. "That's not from another planet. It's an animal called an iguana *(ih GWAH nuh)*."

"Why are its toes so long?" Tony wanted to know.

"To help it walk," Mrs. King said. "It comes from a very dry and sandy place. When an iguana walks, it spreads its long toes. Doing this helps it stay on top of the sand instead of sinking into it."

"Are you sure it's an iguana?" Katie asked. "It sure looks like something from another planet to me!"

THINKING FOCUS

How do plants and animals adjust to living in the desert?

Key Terms

- desert
- climate

The Desert Land

A **desert** is an area where little rain falls and few kinds of plants grow. Katie's iguana, like the one shown here, can be found in the deserts of the southwestern United States. This area includes the states of Arizona, Texas, New Mexico, California, Nevada, Utah, and Colorado. Look for this area on the map on page 52.

Key
Desert

▲ *How does this desert look different from prairies?*

Most deserts are very hot, but not all deserts are the same. Some deserts are hot during the day but cool at night. Many deserts are hot in summer and cold in winter. Hot temperatures and changes from very hot to very cold make it hard for plants to live in deserts.

Temperatures are not the only problem for desert plant life. Little rain falls in deserts, so the soil is very dry. Desert soil is also rocky or sandy. Many plants do not grow well in such soil. Because there are not many plants in the desert, there are few decaying plants to form humus. Humus helps soil hold water. The sandy desert soil dries out quickly even after a hard rain.

Even though a desert is hot and dry and the soil is poor, some plants grow well there. You will see on the next page that the saguaro *(suh GWAHR oh)* cactus has special ways to live in the desert. ■

52 ■ *Why don't many plants grow well in the desert?*

The Saguaro Cactus

10:32 A.M. May 5, 1991
After a spring rain in the
Sonoran Desert in Arizona

Flowers
Raindrops sparkle
on these blossoms
that opened during
the cool night hours.
The flowers will close
again before the
afternoon heat
reaches 110° F.

Elf Owl
The unusual sound of
falling rain woke this
tiny owl from its daytime
sleep. During the day,
the owl hides in this
hole made by a
woodpecker months
ago. At night, it leaves
the nest to hunt

Arm
Sharp thorns cover
the arms that show
that this cactus is
very old. A saguaro
doesn't grow arms
until it's at least 75
years old. Some
saguaros live 250
years. They may
stand 50 feet tall
and have 50 arms.

Woodpecker
A loud tap, tap, tap
fills the desert air as
this bird pecks a hole
in the trunk of the
cactus. Today, it will
find plenty of water
inside. Later, another
bird will build a nest in
this hole.

Trunk
Swollen to twice its
normal size, the trunk is
filled with hundreds of
gallons of rain water. The
saguaro's roots quickly
soaked up the water from
the desert sands.

Jack Rabbit
After nibbling tender
young cactus sprouts in
the early morning, this
rabbit has hopped into
the cool shade of the
saguaro. There it can
avoid the scorching sun
until late afternoon.

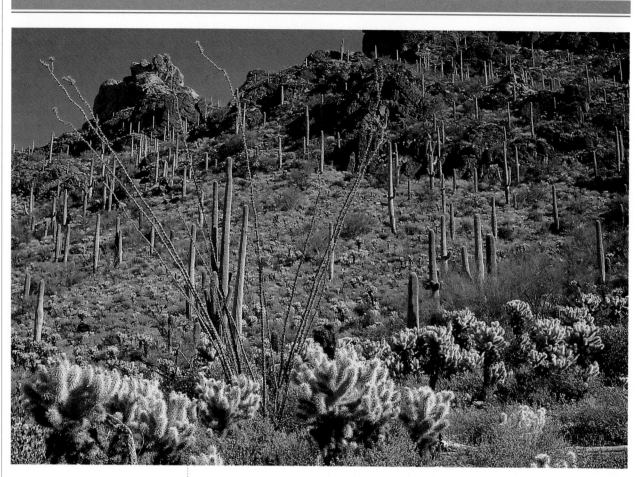

▲ *The desert above is full of different kinds of cactus. Can you find the saguaros?*

▼ *Sagebrush covers the desert below. Like a cactus, sagebrush grows well in very dry soil.*

Life in the Desert

The dry desert climate presents problems for living things. **Climate** is the usual weather of an area over a long time. How do plants and animals live in such a dry climate?

The cactus has a special way of staying alive in the desert. Its long roots spread out around it and are not very deep in the soil. When rain comes, a cactus uses these roots to draw water up into its trunk. The cactus saves the water for use during dry weather.

Animals have their own ways of staying alive in the desert. Many desert animals get much of their water from their food. The little kangaroo rat, for example, gets most of its water from the seeds it eats. Meat also contains water, so predators get water from the animals they eat.

Animals must also find a way to deal with hot desert temperatures. Kangaroo rats dig burrows. The earth is cooler under the desert soil. These animals nest in their burrows during the day. At night when it is cooler, they search for food.

Other animals have different ways of staying comfortable. An iguana crawls into the shade of a rock

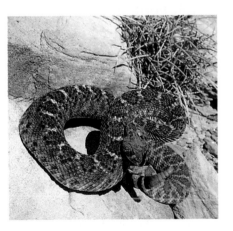

when it gets hot. When the iguana becomes cool, it covers its body with sand. The iguana leaves only its head showing. Snakes stay in underground holes or in the shade of rocks and bushes during hot daylight hours. They come out to hunt for food at night.

Desert life is not easy for plants or animals. However, with their special ways of staying alive, the desert is full of life. ■

▲ *This kangaroo rat never needs to drink water. It gets most of its water from seeds like the ones above.*

◄ *A rattlesnake gets its name from the rattle at the end of its tail. Poison shoots out of the snake's two long fangs when it bites.*

■ *Why is life in the desert hard?*

R E V I E W

1. **FOCUS** How do plants and animals adjust to living in the desert?
2. **CONNECT** How is desert soil different from forest and prairie soil?
3. **CRITICAL THINKING** How is desert life during the day different from desert life during the night?

4. **WRITING ACTIVITY** Pretend you have a friend who thinks that nothing grows in deserts. Write a paragraph that explains why the desert is full of life.

55

The Land Around You

What is the land like where you live? Are there rivers or lakes nearby? Is the land flat or is it hilly? Rivers, lakes, oceans, mountains, and hills are all physical features. You can explore the area where you live to find out more about its physical features.

Get Ready   Begin by looking at the land near where you live. Then look at the land near your school and other places you visit close to home. Start a notebook of the physical features you see around you. Write about what you see. Draw pictures of the land you explore. You can also learn more about the land where you live by looking at maps and photographs.

Find Out   Make a map of your area to show how the land looks. Use the notes and drawings in your notebook for help. You may also use photographs and maps from books and newspapers for help.

I see a river and a hill.

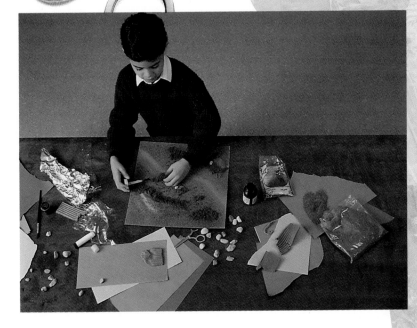

Move Ahead   The map you made is on a flat piece of paper. All the physical features you drew on the map are flat. To show more exactly how the land looks, you can make a model from your map. Build your model with materials that you have at home or in your classroom. Clay and small rocks can be hills or mountains. Aluminum foil or plastic wrap can be rivers or lakes. Can you think of other materials to use?

Explore Some More   Share your model with your classmates and other students in your school. Set up a display in your classroom. Label the models and show the maps you drew. Be ready to answer questions about your model and about the land in your area.

Chapter Review

Reviewing Key Terms

climate (p. 54)   physical feature (p. 45)
desert (p. 51)   temperature (p. 45)
mountain (p. 45)   timberline (p. 45)

A. Write the key term for each meaning.
1. how hot or cold something is
2. the place on a mountain above which trees do not grow
3. the usual weather of an area
4. a land feature that has steep sides and a peak
5. a natural part of the earth's surface
6. an area that gets very little rain

B. Write a complete sentence to answer each question.
1. How are bighorn sheep able to live so well on mountains?
2. What are some of the physical features of the area where you live?
3. What kind of plants grow above the timberline?
4. What is the climate where you live?

Exploring Concepts

A. The chart to the right lists one plant and three animals that live in the desert. Copy the chart and fill in the second column. Your chart will show what the plant and the animals do to stay alive in the desert.

B. Write your answer to each question in one or two sentences.
1. How do high mountains affect the land east of them?
2. Why doesn't desert soil hold rain water well?

Plant or Animal	How it lives in the desert
Cactus	
Kangaroo rat	
Iguana	
Elf owl	

Reviewing Skills

1. Copy the map of Wyoming shown below. Add the mountains, lakes, and rivers. Then make a physical features key for your map. Use the map on pages 238–239 for help.

2. Locate your state on the map on pages 238–239. List the physical features that are in your state.

3. Look at the map on pages 236–237. Choose a state. Write three clues that will help a classmate guess the name of the state you choose. Include a cardinal or intermediate direction in each clue. For example, "To get to this state, you must travel northeast from Texas." Take turns trying to name each other's state.

Wyoming

Using Critical Thinking

1. Air conditioning keeps people cool in hot weather. If there were no electricity, how could you stay comfortable in a very hot climate?

2. High mountains are cold and deserts are hot, but in some ways they are alike. Make a list of the ways they are alike.

3. Would you rather live on a mountain top or in a desert? Why?

Preparing for Citizenship

1. **WRITING ACTIVITY** Pretend you and a partner climbed a high mountain. Tape record your reports about what you took with you and what you saw above the timberline.

2. **COLLABORATIVE LEARNING** Prepare a class bulletin board on desert animals. Work in groups and find books about life in the desert. Some group members can draw pictures of desert animals, such as the desert tortoise and the roadrunner. Some group members can write a sentence or two about each animal. Add your pictures and sentences to the bulletin board.

The Land and the First Americans

The first Americans lived all across the land—by the sea, in the forests, on the prairies, and in the deserts. These Native Americans understood the land and lived from it. They chose their clothing, food, and homes from what nature offered them. Items used every day were not only made from natural materials, they were often colored with natural dyes and decorated with artwork that told stories about the land.

Navajo sand painting blanket of the Nightway Chant, 1880.
Werner Forman Archive/Private Collection, New York.

Chapter 4

By the Shining Sea

Can you imagine eating fish and forest plants almost every day? These were the main foods of a group of people called the Kwakiutl (kwah kee OO duhl). *They lived along the northwest coast of North America. The Kwakiutl depended on the land and sea for all of their needs. In return, these people held celebrations and created beautiful artwork to honor nature.*

Tall totem poles stood in front of many Kwakiutl homes. The Kwakiutl carved wood from the forest into works of art that were used to tell stories of a family's history.

This piece of clothing was worn as a skirt or a cape. It was made out of tree bark at least 100 years ago by Northwest Coast Indians.

The Kwakiutl made large wooden canoes for fishing and traveling. Sometimes they would dress in special costumes and masks to attend celebrations in nearby villages.

Kwakiutl masks showed the faces of creatures from ancient stories. Dancers sometimes acted out these stories during celebrations.

Between Sea and Forest

THINKING FOCUS

How did the Kwakiutl meet their basic need for food and shelter?

Key Terms

- salmon
- cedar
- long house

➤ *This picture of a woman wearing a cedar bark blanket was taken long ago. Below is a wooden beater that women used to pound the bark before it could be woven into blankets or clothing.*

Kwiskwis is very excited! Today her mother will show her how women make clothes out of tree bark.

"Where do we start?" asks Kwiskwis excitedly.

"With a cedar *(SEE dur)* tree," her mother says.

Kwiskwis and her mother pull long strips of bark off the trees. Then they pull the softer inner bark from these strips. When they collect as much of the softer bark as they can carry, they return to their big wooden house.

"First we pound the bark with this beater until it is not so stiff," says Mother. "Next, we will separate the bark into thin strips. We will weave these strips together on this frame to make a new cape for your grandmother."

Kwiskwis smiles, knowing the gift will keep her grandmother warm and dry.

Sea of Plenty

If you could have visited a Kwakiutl village one hundred or more years ago, you might have seen a girl like Kwiskwis and her mother making clothes from tree bark. The Kwakiutl were one of many Indian groups that lived along the northwest coast of North America. These northwest coast groups lived on a strip of land that stretches from the southern tip of Alaska all the way to northern California. Look at the map. Notice that the Kwakiutl lived in what is now Canada.

Remember what you learned about oceans and forests in Chapters 1 and 2? The Kwakiutl lived in thick forests between the ocean and the high mountains.

Water Provides Food

Water played a large part in the way the Kwakiutl lived. The Pacific Ocean and nearby rivers provided plenty of fish to eat, such as trout, halibut, and **salmon** (SA muhn). The Kwakiutl also ate small seafood, such as clams, and large sea animals, such as seals. However, salmon was their favorite food.

The Kwakiutl believed that all things in nature lived in order to help each other. Each year the salmon left the ocean and swam upstream past Kwakiutl villages to lay their eggs. The Kwakiutl thought these fish swam upstream to feed the villagers.

The Kwakiutl wanted to be sure that the salmon would come back each year. When they ate salmon, they always saved the bones. Then they would return the bones to the

▼ Kwakiutl villages were near plentiful water resources—the water of rivers, streams, and the ocean.

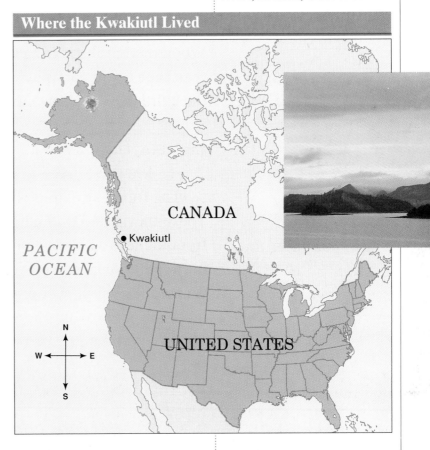

Where the Kwakiutl Lived

CANADA

PACIFIC OCEAN

• Kwakiutl

UNITED STATES

N
W E
S

> ➤ *The Kwakiutl made fish hooks from wood. First, they heated the wood with steam. Then they bent it to form a hook.*

■ *How did living near water affect Kwakiutl life?*

▼ *This wooden box is fitted together and tied with cedar bark rope. Boxes were used for seats and shelves. They were also used to hold food, water, and family treasures.*

water where the fish had been caught. They believed those fish would get new bodies and come again the next year.

The Kwakiutl ate fish more than any other food, and they became very good at fishing. The Kwakiutl caught fish with hooks made of wood, bone, or horn. They also used spears and nets. When the Kwakiutl caught more than they could eat, they would dry the extra fish. This gave them food for the winter. ■

Forest Gifts

The forest also helped the Kwakiutl meet their needs. There they could find berries and animals to eat. Wood from the forest was even more important to them. They lived in houses made of wood and traveled in wooden canoes. They used wood to make chests, dishes, toys, bows, arrows, and more.

Cedar was the type of wood used most often by the Kwakiutl. A **cedar** is a type of evergreen tree. The Kwakiutl used cedar's soft inner bark to make rope, mats, and clothing. Sometimes they would weave cedar bark and mountain goat wool together to make warm blankets.

The Kwakiutl were careful not to pull too much bark from a cedar tree. They knew that this could kill the tree. The Kwakiutl believed that cedar trees, like the salmon, were there to help them. Sometimes they sang a song to the cedar, asking it to clothe and shelter them. Then they thanked the tree for giving them so much.

Cedar was the Kwakiutl's favorite wood for building houses. These houses were called **long houses.** They were up to 60 feet long. The Kwakiutl split logs into thin boards to make the walls and roof. Some roof boards could be moved to let out smoke from the cooking fires.

◄ *The artist has drawn this so you can see the inside of a long house. How many different ways do they use wood in this picture?*

Three or four related families usually shared a long house. Each family had its own space and cooking fire in one corner of the house. Kwakiutl long houses were all built close together in a row, facing the sea.

The Kwakiutl cared about nature. They felt that the land and sea gave them many things. The Kwakiutl took only what they needed and gave back what they could. ■

■ *How did forests help the Kwakiutl?*

R E V I E W

1. **FOCUS** How did the Kwakiutl meet their basic need for food and shelter?
2. **CONNECT** From what you know about oceans and rivers, where did the Kwakiutl get their freshwater fish?
3. **CRITICAL THINKING** The Kwakiutl believed that all things in nature lived to help each other. How did this affect the way the Kwakiutl treated nature?
4. **ACTIVITY** Draw a picture that shows how the Kwakiutl used either the sea or the forest in their everyday lives.

Using Timelines

Here's Why   It is not easy to keep track of all the events we read about. Timelines can help. A timeline shows events in the order in which they happened. Some timelines show events for a short period of time, such as a week. Many timelines, however, cover more than one year. Years are shown on those timelines. Suppose you wanted to show certain events in the life of a Kwakiutl boy named Weesa.

Here's How   You read most timelines from left to right. Events that took place earlier in time are shown on the left side of the timeline. Events that happened later are shown on the right.

Events in Weesa's Life

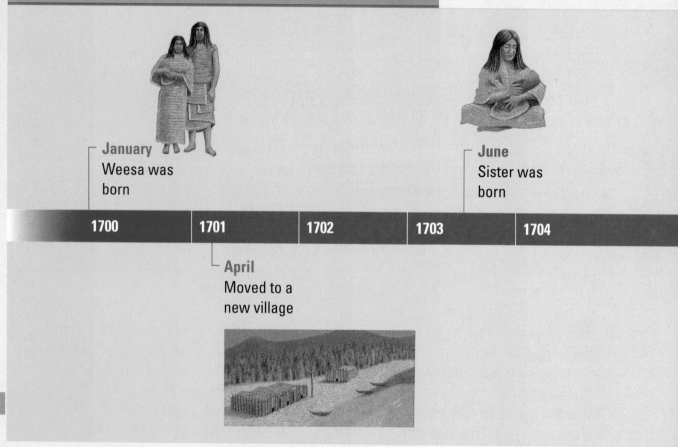

January
Weesa was born

June
Sister was born

| 1700 | 1701 | 1702 | 1703 | 1704 |

April
Moved to a new village

68

Look at the left side of the timeline below. What happened to Weesa in the year 1700? Notice that dates are shown by years on the timeline. What happened to Weesa in the year 1701? How old was he then? How old was he when his sister was born?

Try It You can learn many things about the Kwakiutl boy's life by looking at the timeline. In what year did Weesa help his father carve a mask? Was that before or after he went to the totem-pole raising? How old was Weesa when he helped his father carve a mask? What is the latest date that is shown on the timeline? What happened that year?

Apply It Make a timeline of your life. Start on the left with the year you were born. Then write the year it is now at the right. Show five or six events on your timeline in the order in which they happened. Draw pictures of some of the events on your timeline.

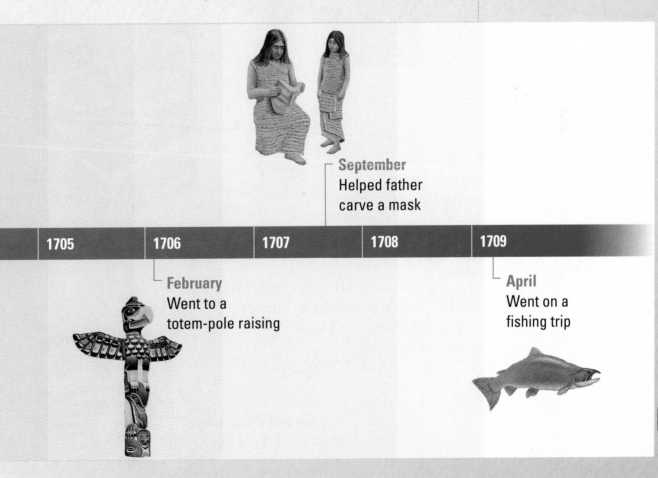

September
Helped father
carve a mask

| 1705 | 1706 | 1707 | 1708 | 1709 |

February
Went to a
totem-pole raising

April
Went on a
fishing trip

Of Art and Wood

How was wood important to the Kwakiutl?

Key Terms

- totem pole
- ceremony

The Indians of the northwest coast were some of the best woodworkers in North America. They carved animals on many of the things they made. An artist chose certain parts of an animal to carve.

The large front teeth and the wide, flat tail show that this is a beaver.

Big claws help to show that this is a bear.

This animal has large teeth and fins. It also blows air through a hole on the top of its head. It is a killer whale.

What parts of this drawing help to show it is a frog?

Totem Poles and Canoes

Animals like the ones on page 70 were carved into many Kwakiutl objects. Almost everything the Kwakiutl used was made of wood. Carving was an important part of Kwakiutl life.

Remember that Kwakiutl women were weavers. Kwakiutl men were woodcarvers. They taught their sons this skill. If a boy grew up to be a good carver, he became an important person in a Kwakiutl village.

Kwakiutl woodcarvers made beautiful totem poles. A **totem pole** is a wooden pole decorated with figures that showed a family's history. A Kwakiutl totem pole could be 10 to 70 feet tall. Each figure on it stood for an animal, a person, or an event in a family's history.

One of the biggest jobs for a woodcarver was making a canoe like the one shown below. First, he cut down a tall cedar tree and chopped it into the shape of a canoe. Then he used hot stones to burn out the inside of the log. He chipped away the burned parts to form the inside of the canoe.

The Kwakiutl still carve totem poles today. In 1980, Kwakiutl carvers in Canada created a totem pole as tall as an eight-story building.

▼ This colorful Kwakiutl totem pole stands in Canada today. Can you name any of the figures on it?

71

Next, the woodcarver put water into the canoe. He added very hot stones to make steam. The steam softened the wood. Once the sides were soft, they could be stretched. Bigger and bigger sticks were forced between the two sides until the opening was big enough to fit many people in the canoe. A finished canoe could be 50 feet long and hold 40 people.

Finally, like most Kwakiutl items, many canoes were carved and painted. Even Kwakiutl boats became works of art. ■

■ *How did the Kwakiutl use wood in everyday life?*

Special Ceremonies

The Kwakiutl celebrated important events such as weddings or births. There were special words, actions, and songs for each event. The way people act during such important events is called a **ceremony.** Kwakiutl ceremonies were full of dancing, storytelling, and feasting.

The Kwakiutl used finely carved masks, rattles, and puppets during ceremonies. These pieces of art showed animals of the land, water, and air. They were used to tell stories about families and nature.

➤ *The Kwakiutl in this picture are wearing costumes that they wore during ceremonies. During these ceremonies, they might have used a rattle like the one pictured below.*

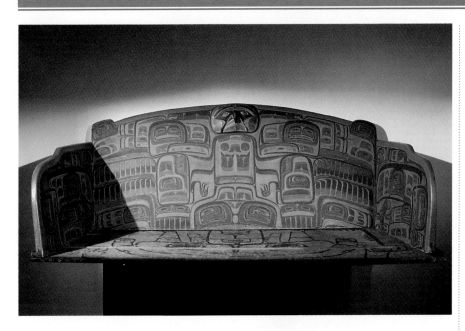

◄ *During Kwakiutl ceremonies, a chief would sit in a wooden seat like this one.*

How Do We Know?

There are no old totem poles left today, since wood decays quickly in forests. We know that totem poles were carved by northwest coast groups as long as 200 years ago, because a French visitor described one in his journal.

One Kwakiutl ceremony was a totem-pole raising. A totem-pole raising was held on many special occasions, such as weddings and funerals. Sometimes a family raised a totem pole to call attention to something brave a family member had done.

Not all Kwakiutl families had totem poles. Totem poles showed a family's importance in the community. A family had to be important and rich enough to have one made.

A totem pole was usually set up in front of a house. During the totem-pole raising, a family would gather near the totem pole. In a loud voice, the head of the family would tell stories about his family's past.

The speechmaker used the figures on the totem pole to remind him of his family's story. For example, the carving of a sea lion on the pole might remind him of an important event that happened long ago.

A totem-pole raising was an important event. The speechmaker, like the one on the next page, wore special clothes to tell his family's story. People outside of the family were allowed to hear the story, but only a family member was allowed to tell it.

⋏ *Even from far away, a Kwakiutl could tell who lived in this house. The totem pole is like a sign that tells which family lives there.*

73

A Kwakiutl Speechmaker

5:06 P.M., October 20, 1843
In front of a long house on
the northwest coast

Talking Stick
A whale's tail is carved into this stick. The day the speechmaker was born, his mother saw a whale's tail flashing in the sea. Now it is a sign of his family's strength.

Neck Ring
The speechmaker wears this colorful ring made from red cedar bark. He last wore it at his daughter's wedding.

Copper
His thoughts are far from a fight, but the speechmaker is proudly holding a shield called a copper. It is so valuable that he could trade it for 2,500 blankets.

Blanket
The blanket that drapes the speechmaker's shoulders is made from cedar bark and the hair of a mountain goat.

◄ *This mask was worn during Kwakiutl ceremonies by a dancer who opened and closed the bird's mouth to make a loud snapping sound. The bird was an evil creature in Kwakiutl myths.*

Totem-pole raisings were not the only Kwakiutl ceremonies. The winter days in Kwakiutl villages were filled with the sounds of singing, dancing, speeches, and feasting. Often performers wearing large wooden masks acted out stories of spirits in nature. The masks were carved and painted to look like these spirits. They added to the excitement of Kwakiutl winter ceremonies.

◄ *This mask shows the face of a feared giant in Kwakiutl myths. It is made from wood and human hair. At one time it had thick eyebrows and a mustache and beard made from bear fur.*

The Kwakiutl had more time for ceremonies in the winter because they didn't spend as much time gathering food. During the warmer days, they caught more fish than they could use. They dried some of these fish to eat during the winter. This gave the Kwakiutl time during the winter for their ceremonies. ■

■ *How did the Kwakiutl use wood in their ceremonies?*

R E V I E W

1. **FOCUS** How was wood important to the Kwakiutl?
2. **CONNECT** How would Kwakiutl life have been different if these people had lived in a desert?
3. **CRITICAL THINKING** How did the Kwakiutl's ideas about nature affect their art and ceremonies?
4. **WRITING ACTIVITY** Choose an animal from land, sea, or air. Make a drawing of it like the Kwakiutl figures on page 70. Write a short story that a speechmaker might tell about your animal.

Chapter Review

Reviewing Key Terms

cedar (p. 66)   salmon (p. 65)
ceremony (p. 72)   totem pole (p. 71)
long house (p. 67)

A. Write the key term for each meaning.
1. a carved, wooden pole owned by a family
2. a kind of evergreen tree
3. a fish that lives in the Pacific Ocean and swims up rivers to lay eggs
4. a wooden house up to 60 feet long

B. Copy the story below. Change one word in each sentence to make the sentences correct.

Long ago, a Kwakiutl girl lived in a tent with her family. They ate hamburgers for dinner. Her father took her for rides in a boat made of bamboo. Her family had their own flagpole. They celebrated important events with a game.

Exploring Concepts

A. The chart below shows where the Kwakiutl found many useful things. Copy the chart. Fill in the last two columns to show what was used and how it was used.

B. Write two details to support each of the following main ideas.
1. The Kwakiutl took only what they needed from nature.
2. The Kwakiutl made beautiful things.

Where	What was used	How it was used
Forest		
River or ocean		

Reviewing Skills

1. Copy the timeline of a week below. On your timeline, mark the days you go to school, the days you stay home, and the days you have something special planned.

2. Look at the map on page 65 again. What body of water lies west of where the Kwakiutl lived? What state lies north of where the Kwakiutl lived?

Timeline for a Week

School

Monday	Tuesday	Wednesday	Thursday	Friday	Saturday	Sunday

Using Critical Thinking

1. The Kwakiutl used wood from the forest in many ways. How would a forest fire have changed their lives?

2. The Kwakiutl were fine artists and spent long hours making beautiful things. Name some types of art that people today spend a long time making.

3. Compare a Kwakiutl family's totem pole to a family's photo album today. How are they alike?

Preparing for Citizenship

1. **ART ACTIVITY** Work with a partner. Write a story about a Kwakiutl family. Tell something they did or something that happened to them. Then, make a totem pole by rolling and pasting cardboard or heavy paper into a long tube. Decorate your totem pole to match your story.

2. **COLLABORATIVE LEARNING** With your class, have a totem-pole raising. Choose speechmakers to tell the family stories shown on the totem poles you made. Others in the class can make paper neck rings and talking sticks. Gather together to listen to the stories.

Chapter 5

Over Waves of Grass

Finding food was not an easy task for the Cheyenne (shy AN) people. Unlike the Kwakiutl, who had plenty of fish nearby, the Cheyenne had to work hard for their food. Hundreds of years ago, they spent most of their time farming to grow food. Later they had horses and hunted buffalo for meat.

The buffalo lived on the plains in huge herds. The Cheyenne depended on this great beast for food, clothing, and even shelter.

Buffalo hides had many uses. Sometimes the Cheyenne would decorate hides with drawings that told stories of important events, such as hunts or celebrations.

This Cheyenne woman follows the ways of her ancestors.

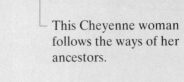

The Cheyenne used buffalo leather bags to hold many things. This bag is about 200 years old.

Following the Buffalo

Key Terms

- tipi
- natural resource

➤ *This is part of a painting called* Tall Tales on a Full Stomach. *It was painted in 1985 by Paladine Roye, a Native American artist.*

Black Kettle licked buffalo grease from his lips and sighed happily. He looked at the other Cheyenne sitting around the campfire and knew they felt the same way. Their stomachs had not been full for a long time.

Black Kettle knew how it felt to be hungry. The crops had failed to grow this summer. At night, he dreamed about food. Often, he listened to his uncles tell stories about hunger. He wondered how long it would be before they would have another buffalo feast. Hunting buffalo on foot was hard work. His people had followed one herd for almost a week before they got close enough to shoot this buffalo. Even then, the men had been almost too weak from hunger to lift their bows for the kill.

Buffalo Herds in 1600

Key
■ Buffalo herds, 1600

ATLANTIC OCEAN

N W E S

▲ *The Plains Indians used arrowpoints like these to hunt buffalo as long as two thousand years ago. They were chipped into points with bone or stone tools.*

The Great Provider

If you were a Cheyenne living about 400 years ago, you might have eaten a feast like the one Black Kettle ate. Your family would have farmed and often hunted buffalo in the vast area shown on the map above. The Cheyenne were one of many groups of Plains Indians.

Growing beans, corn, and squash on the plains was difficult. The earth was tough to dig into for planting, and was often dry. If it rained enough, and the Cheyenne had a good harvest, they would eat well. If harvests were small, the Cheyenne hunted whatever animals they could find, such as deer and rabbits. Even so, there often wasn't enough to eat.

Several times during the year, the Cheyenne would leave their homes to hunt buffalo. They camped along the way in tipis *(TEE peez)*. **Tipis** are cone-shaped tents that can be put up and taken down quickly.

To the Cheyenne, the buffalo was a great provider, an important **natural resource**. A natural resource is anything found in nature that helps people live. ■

Across Time & Space

The Cheyenne moved about for a long time. Today, the Cheyenne people are divided into two groups and no longer move. The Northern Cheyenne live in Montana. The Southern Cheyenne live in Oklahoma. Find these states on the United States map on pages 234–235 in the Atlas.

■ *Why was farming on the plains so difficult for the Cheyenne?*

81

The Great Provider

The buffalo was an important source of food for the Cheyenne. A single buffalo could provide enough meat to feed a hundred people. Everything was used. Nothing was wasted. Today we use softened cowhide to make things we use every day, just as the Cheyenne used buffalo hide.

Tipi walls were hides sewn together with a buffalo-bone needle, and thread that was also made from part of the buffalo. The hides were stretched over wooden poles.

Rib bones were tied together with buffalo-hide string to make sleds for moving camp in the snow, or for some winter fun!

Buffalo fat was mixed with dried meat, acorns, pine nuts, chokecherries, and honey to make pemmican *(PEHM ih kuhn)*. Pemmican was a healthy food they could eat anytime.

Cheyenne women stretched and dried buffalo hides before using them. Look at the buffalo meat drying on racks in the sun. Dried meat could be kept and eaten during the winter.

Shoes became works of art when leather moccasins were decorated with beads. The Cheyenne also made dresses, capes, shirts, and warm robes from buffalo hides.

Help from the Horse

Picture loading all your belongings onto your back! That's what the Cheyenne did when they hunted buffalo. Everyone went on the hunt—grandparents, parents, and children. Women carried the babies and heavy loads. Men carried bows and arrows, in case an animal might run by. Families tied their bundles onto poles pulled by dogs.

Using dogs to travel wasn't easy. They chased rabbits, got into fights, even took naps! Traveling was so slow the Cheyenne moved only five or six miles a day. It was hard to chase buffalo at that speed!

Then the life of the Cheyenne became easier. About 250 years ago, they got horses from their Spanish and Indian neighbors to the south. As the Cheyenne learned to raise their own horses, they became skillful riders. Now hunters could keep up with the herds. Also, horses could pull heavier loads and travel faster than dogs.

Thanks to the horse, the Cheyenne stopped farming. They moved about freely, setting up new camps along the way as they followed the buffalo all year long. The Cheyenne were rarely hungry again. ■

▼ *Cheyenne men pose with their horses that brought them, their tipis, and their families to a summer celebration on the plains.*

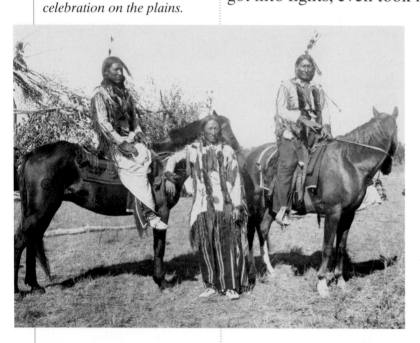

■ *Find details to support this statement: The horse made life easier for the Cheyenne.*

R E V I E W

1. **FOCUS** How did the Cheyenne depend on the buffalo?
2. **CONNECT** Remember what you learned about prairies. Do you think the Cheyenne had trouble finding wooden poles to put up the tipi? Why?
3. **CRITICAL THINKING** If you had to move around all the time to search for food, do you think you would keep a lot of things? Why?
4. **ACTIVITY** Imagine that you are a Cheyenne. Tear a piece of brown craft paper so that it looks like a buffalo hide. Draw an important scene from your life.

We Use Natural Resources

The Cheyenne used the buffalo to provide food, clothing, and shelter. The buffalo were a natural resource. A natural resource is anything found in nature that people can use.

Trees, soil, and water were also natural resources for the Cheyenne. The poles that dogs dragged behind them and that held up Cheyenne tipis came from trees. The Cheyenne raised crops in the soil and drank water from streams.

Today, we use many of the same natural resources. We use trees to make everything from houses to paper to clothing. We also use the soil to grow food. We drink water that comes from rivers, lakes, and underground wells.

Natural resources are also found inside the earth. Things like oil, coal, rocks, and metals are natural resources. Today, we use oil to make gasoline for cars. We burn coal in factories, and we use rocks to make cement sidewalks. We build many things, such as cars, with metals. These resources are as important to us as the buffalo were to the Cheyenne.

The Medicine Dance

Why was the Medicine Dance important to the Cheyenne?

Key Terms

- myth
- symbol

Long ago, no rain had fallen on the land for many days. Grass died and animals starved. There was nothing to eat.

One day, a Cheyenne man and woman set out on a journey. They traveled for many days until they came to a tree-covered mountain. They pushed aside a rock that hid a cave. Inside, they saw an amazing room! Above and around them were wooden poles covered with buffalo robes. In the center stood a tree trunk with a nest of the magical Thunderbird at its top.

Then they heard the deep voice of the spirit Roaring Thunder. Roaring Thunder told the man and woman how to perform a dance. The dance would bring life back to the grasses of the earth and would bring herds of buffalo back to the people.

Cheyenne myth, retold

➤ *This Indian drum shows the Thunderbird. Many groups of Plains Indians believed that the Thunderbird controlled wind, rain, and snow.*

The Cycle of Nature

This myth tells how the Cheyenne ceremony called the Medicine Dance began. A **myth** is a story that explains something in nature. This myth was the Cheyenne's way of explaining nature as changes that repeat over and over. We call this repeating pattern the cycle of nature.

To understand this cycle, think about a tree. In the spring, green leaves sprout. The tree grows all summer. In the fall, its leaves turn colors and fall off. During the winter, the tree looks almost dead. When spring comes, new buds appear. Then the cycle begins again.

The Cheyenne saw this cycle all around them. Each year the prairie grass grew and died, the buffalo came and went. The Cheyenne believed there were great powers in nature. They thought of these powers as medicine that could help people. The Cheyenne held a Medicine Dance to get help from these powers.

▼ *Scientists think that Indians from the plains may have held Medicine Dances on this circle called a medicine wheel. It is in Medicine Mountain, Wyoming.*

All the Cheyenne people would arrange their tipis in a huge circle for the eight-day ceremony. A Cheyenne couple took the part of the man and woman in the myth on page 86. The man was a medicine man. The Cheyenne believed that a medicine man could talk with the powers of nature, such as Roaring Thunder.

The Cheyenne saw everything around them as part of the cycle of nature. All living things begin, grow, and die, but new ones take their place. When the Cheyenne celebrated the Medicine Dance, they were trying to make sure that the cycle of nature would continue. They believed that acting out this myth would help bring new life to the grasses, and would bring herds of buffalo back to the people. ■

■ Why was the cycle of nature important to the Cheyenne?

➤ These Cheyenne are ready for a Medicine Dance.

The Medicine Dance Tent

➤ This leather rattle was used during Medicine Dance ceremonies. It may have been used by the Cheyenne to make a sound like running buffalo.

During the Medicine Dance celebration, the Cheyenne made a tent that looked like the mountain room in the myth. In it, they put up a tree like the tree in that room. The tree was the most important symbol in the Medicine Dance. A **symbol** is something that stands for something else. The tree was a symbol of the way life changes and begins again.

The Cheyenne would pick out a special cottonwood tree. Before cutting it down, the chief gave a speech, saying that the tree was a symbol of nature.

After the Cheyenne cut down the tree and removed its branches, they decorated the top of it with branches and leaves. Women placed bits of brightly colored cloth on the branches. The tree then looked like the nest of the mighty Thunderbird. The nest reminded the Cheyenne of Roaring Thunder because they believed that this spirit flew through the sky in the shape of the Thunderbird.

Next, the Cheyenne put up the decorated tree in the middle of a round tent they had built. The tent was made of a circle of poles tied together. Buffalo robes covered the sides and part of the roof. Standing out from the top of the finished tent was the tree with its nest.

Finally, the dancing began. For the last two days of the ceremony, the Cheyenne would feast and dance around the pole. They celebrated the cycle of nature. ■

■ *How did the Cheyenne use symbols in their celebration of the Medicine Dance?*

Building a Medicine Dance Tent

Step One: Poles are put into a circle with an opening facing east.

Step Two: Leaves, branches, and bits of cloth are attached to a tree trunk. This center pole is raised.

Step Three: Buffalo robes are attached to the sides and part of the roof. Now the dance begins.

R E V I E W

1. **FOCUS** Why was the Medicine Dance important to the Cheyenne?

2. **CONNECT** How are Cheyenne ideas about nature like Kwakiutl ideas about nature?

3. **CRITICAL THINKING** Use an acorn to describe the cycle of nature.

4. **ACTIVITY** Create your own tree from a cardboard tube. Decorate it and add paper branches and leaves to make a Thunderbird nest. Add bits of colored paper to decorate its branches.

The First American People

Try to imagine what your neighborhood was like a long, long time ago. There were no large houses, or wide streets, or busy highways. There were hundreds of different groups of Indian people who first lived in North America. These groups had different names and their own ways of living. Some of them lived where you live today.

Get Ready In a few places, Native Americans still live where they always did. In other places, you can see what's left of Indian homes. In most places, though, little is left to tell about these early people. How can you learn about the Indians who lived in your area?

Find Out Begin by looking at books and maps to find the names of the Indians who lived in

▲ *Cliff Palace in Mesa Verde National Park, Colorado.*

➤ *Wichita Indian lodges made of logs and earth.*

your area. Then read about how they lived, what they ate, what clothes they wore, and what their homes looked like. Write what you learn in a notebook.

Move Ahead   Give a report to your classmates. Tell the most interesting facts you discovered about the Indians in your area. Draw pictures to show how they lived. Show photos from the books you looked at.

Explore Some More   Set up a history center about the Indians who lived in your area. Display your reports and the pictures you drew. Make a poster with a list of places in your area that have names from these people. Make a model of their homes or make something they used, like a basket or a mask. Invite other students in your school to visit your history center.

The Cherokee lived near us in Georgia

This is Sequoyah. He invented the Cherokee alphabet

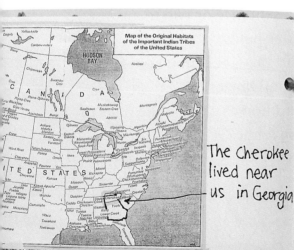

These are masks. They are used in a special dance to help make sick people feel better. This one is like a buffalo head.

The name Cherokee means "real people"

Chapter Review

Reviewing Key Terms

myth (p. 87)   symbol (p. 88)
natural resource (p. 81)   tipi (p. 81)

A. Write the key term that best completes each sentence.
1. Something found in nature that people can use is a _____.
2. A _____ is a cone-shaped tent.
3. Something that stands for something else is a _____.
4. A _____ is a story that explains something in nature.

B. Write *true* or *false* for each sentence below. If a sentence is false, rewrite it to make it true.
1. Myths were important in the life of the Cheyenne.
2. To the Cheyenne, a tree was a symbol of the way life changes.
3. Tipis can be put up and taken down quickly.
4. All natural resources are found above ground.

Exploring Concepts

A. The buffalo was very important to the Cheyenne. It supplied food and was used to make clothing and homes. Copy the cluster diagram below. Fill in the empty spaces. Your diagram will show how the Cheyenne used the buffalo.

B. Write a sentence or two to answer the questions below.
1. Why did the Cheyenne hold the Medicine Dances?
2. How did horses change the lives of the Cheyenne?

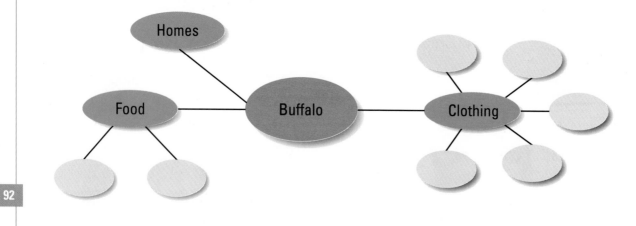

Reviewing Skills

1. The line graph at the right shows how much water was used in a town during a six-month period. In which of the six months was the most water used? In which month was the least used? How many thousand gallons of water were used in July?

2. Look at the map on page 81. Then look at the map on pages 238–239. What physical features are part of the land where the Cheyenne hunted buffalo?

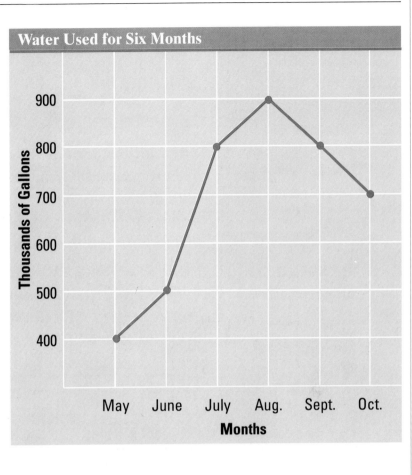

Water Used for Six Months

Thousands of Gallons

900
800
700
600
500
400

May June July Aug. Sept. Oct.

Months

Using Critical Thinking

1. When the Cheyenne moved from place to place, they tied their belongings to poles which were pulled by dogs or horses. How do we move our belongings from place to place today?

2. The Cheyenne were not able to grow as many crops as they needed. How might they have improved their farming?

Preparing for Citizenship

1. **ART ACTIVITY** Draw and color pictures to show the cycle of nature. You should have one picture for each of the four seasons.

2. **COLLABORATIVE LEARNING** As a class project, make a model of the Cheyenne gathering for a Medicine Dance ceremony. Your model should have tipis in a large circle around the Medicine Dance tent. Use straws, clay, colored paper, and other materials you can find.

Chapter 6

In Red Rock Country

The southwestern deserts do not have oceans alive with fish, or prairies covered with thundering herds of buffalo. The deserts are hot, dry lands where it is difficult to find the resources needed to live. The Navajo (NAV uh hoh) people, however, discovered many ways to find the food, clothing, and shelter they needed from their red rock country.

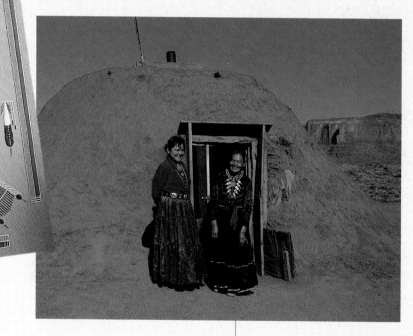

Through sand paintings, the Navajo told stories about nature. The beautiful colors of this painting were made from crushed rock and dried plants.

The mud that covers the outside of Navajo homes has always helped protect the people from winter cold and summer heat.

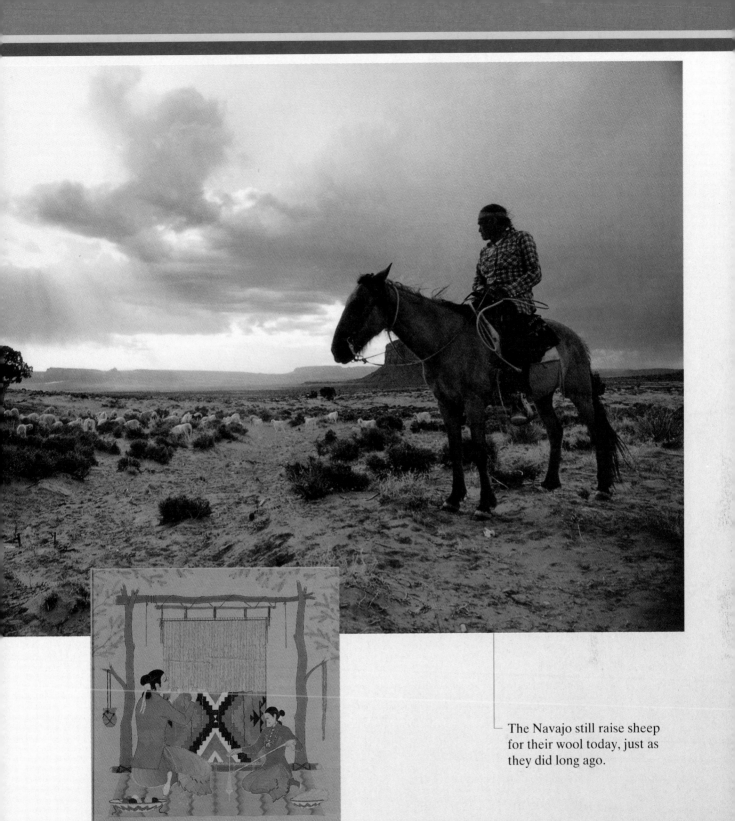

The Navajo still raise sheep for their wool today, just as they did long ago.

This painting, called *Navajo Weavers,* shows how women have woven wool rugs and blankets for hundreds of years.

You have read how the desert can be a harsh place to live. How do the people who live there feel about it? Read this excerpt from a book-length poem to find out who calls the desert theirs.

LITERATURE

THE DESERT IS THEIRS

Written by Byrd Baylor

Illustrated by Peter Parnall

This is no place
for anyone
who wants
soft hills
and meadows
and everything
green
green
green . . .

It's for them.

This is for hawks
that like only
the loneliest canyons
and lizards
that run
in the hottest sand
and
coyotes
that choose
the rockiest trails.

And for
birds
that nest
in cactus
and sing out over
a thousand thorns
because
they're where
they want to be.

It's for them.

And for
hard skinny plants
that do without water
for months
at a time.

And it's for
strong brown Desert People
who call the earth
their mother.

They *have* to see
mountains
and *have* to see
deserts
every day . . .
or they don't feel right.

They wouldn't leave
even for rivers
or flowers
or bending grass.
They'd miss
the sand too much.
They'd miss
the sun.

So
it's for them.

Talk to Papago Indians.
They're
Desert People.

They know
desert secrets
that no one else
knows.

Ask
how they live
in a place
so harsh and dry.

They'll say
they *like*
the land they live on
so they treat it well—
the way you'd treat
an old friend.
They sing it songs.
They never hurt it.

And the land knows.

A Desert Homeland

THINKING
FOCUS

How did the Navajo use the natural resources of the land?

Key Terms

- hogan
- livestock
- adaptation

I see the Earth.
I am looking at Her and smile
Because She makes me happy.
The Earth, looking back at me
is smiling too.
May I walk happily
And lightly
on Her.

Ancient Navajo prayer

This prayer is one of many Navajo prayers about the earth. The Navajo called the earth Changing Woman. Changing Woman was one of the most important spirits in Navajo myths. The Navajo believed that she took care of them in many ways.

➤ *This Navajo is riding through Valley of the Gods in Utah. This area is called red rock country because of the color of the earth.*

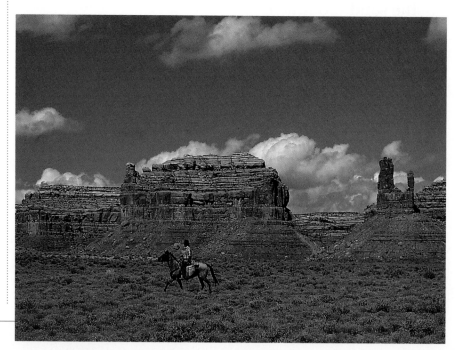

Living Close to the Earth

One of the ways the Navajo believed Changing Woman helped them was by giving them the first hogan. A **hogan** is a one-room house. Navajo have lived in hogans for hundreds of years. In Navajo myths, Changing Woman's hogan was made of shells and turquoise (*TUR kwoyz*), a blue-green stone. When the Navajo made hogans, they made them from mud and logs.

The Navajo lived in the deserts of the southwestern United States. Hogans were good houses for desert living. The mud walls and roofs kept hogans cool in summer and warm in winter. A hogan did not have windows, and the doorway faced east toward the rising sun.

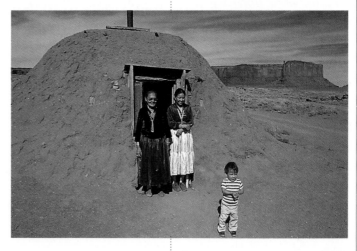

▼ *This Navajo family is standing in front of a hogan in Monument Valley, Utah.*

One family lived in each hogan. Women sat on the north side of a hogan. Men sat on the south side. The west side, the side that faced the doorway, was saved for guests.

In the center of the hogan was a fire that was used for cooking. There was a hole in the roof above the fire to let out smoke. At night a family slept on sheepskins around the fire. ■

■ *How did hogans help the Navajo stay comfortable in the desert?*

Borrowing from Others

The Navajo had many myths to explain changes in their lives. For example, the Navajo believed that Changing Woman, the spirit who gave them hogans, also taught them how to grow corn. Actually, hundreds of years ago, the Navajo learned how to grow corn from another group of Indians. They probably also learned how to grow beans and squash from these people.

How did the Navajo raise corn and other crops in the dry deserts of the Southwest? They learned to farm near streams so that they would have water for their plants.

Corn became very important to the Navajo. They used it in many of their ceremonies because they believed it brought good luck and a long and healthy life.

The Gift of Weaving

The Navajo also believed that weaving was a gift from a spirit. Their myths said Spider Woman taught them to weave. She lived in a tall, thin rock called Spider Rock. This rock still stands in what is now Arizona.

Neighboring Indians that had taught the Navajo to grow crops also taught them to weave cotton. The Navajo quickly improved on this way of weaving. They discovered that wool was even better than cotton for weaving. Wool was stronger and easier to dye, or color.

The Navajo were well known for their beautiful weaving. They began making wool cloth by shearing, or shaving, the wool from the sheep they had raised. Then they spun this wool into yarn. They used natural resources of the earth, such as plants and berries, to dye the wool. Then they wove the wool on a wooden loom. Before long, they had a beautiful piece of cloth to make into clothing or blankets.

Raising Animals

Soon after the Navajo learned to weave, they learned how to raise livestock. Animals, such as sheep or horses, that are raised to be used or traded are called **livestock.** The

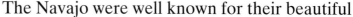

The Navajo are known for their fine weaving. Early Navajo left a hole in each blanket they wove to thank Spider Woman for the gift of weaving. They quit making these holes when they began selling blankets to traders.

▼ *The Navajo still live in the Southwest today. They are the largest group of Native Americans.*

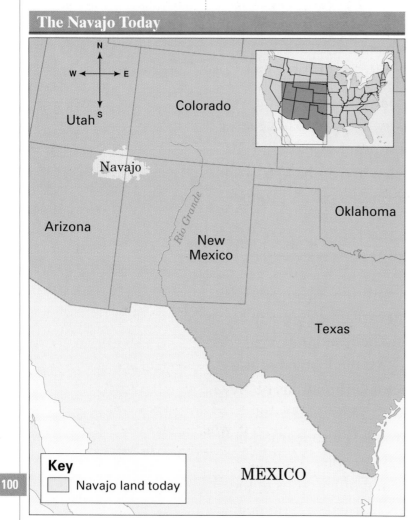

The Navajo Today

N
W — E
S

Utah

Colorado

Navajo

Rio Grande

Arizona

New Mexico

Oklahoma

Texas

MEXICO

Key
☐ Navajo land today

1. Raise sheep   **2.** Shear sheep   **3.** Spin wool into yarn

4. Dye yarn   **5.** Weave yarn on loom   **6.** Finished blanket

Navajo needed sheep so that they would have wool for weaving. They also raised goats and horses.

The way in which the Navajo learned to live in the desert is an example of adaptation. When people change the way they live to fit their surroundings, it is called **adaptation.** The Navajo used natural resources and ideas from others to live well in the desert. ■

■ *What skills did the Navajo learn from their neighbors?*

R E V I E W

1. **FOCUS** How did the Navajo use the natural resources of the land?
2. **CONNECT** How are Navajo hogans different from Kwakiutl long houses and Cheyenne tipis?
3. **CRITICAL THINKING** Why did the Navajo use the name Spider Woman for the spirit who taught them to weave?

4. **WRITING ACTIVITY** Pretend you are sitting inside a Navajo hogan. Write a description of the hogan. Describe its shape and where people are sitting. Draw a picture to go with your description.

We Adapt to Our Surroundings

At one time, the Navajo hunted animals for food. They made clothes from the skins of those animals. When they moved to the hot and dry desert, the Navajo could not find enough wild animals for food and clothing. They had to learn to raise their own animals. They learned how to weave animal hair to make clothing. They also learned how to grow crops, such as corn, beans, and squash. Changing the way we live to fit our surroundings, as the Navajo did, is called adaptation.

Adaptation still takes place today. For example, if you move from Florida to Alaska, you will have to change the way you dress. You will need warmer clothing in Alaska.

Adaptation also happens when people change their surroundings. For example, many people who live in hot climates keep cool by using air conditioning. Farmers in dry climates give their crops water to help them grow, as in the picture below of round corn fields in Kansas.

People often adapt to their surroundings. They change the way they live or they change the area around them.

Sand Painting

Apink sunrise colored the sky as we reached the hogan. My teacher, the medicine man, was quiet. He was thinking about the sick girl he had come to help. The girl's worried family and friends waited outside as we entered. Kneeling beside her, he closed his eyes. Then he began to sing the words of a ceremony used to treat her sickness. The words retold a myth of our people.

Years before, my teacher was a helper like me. He had learned the words from his teacher, a great medicine man who knew hundreds of **chants,** or prayers that are sung. I knew that, in a while, he would finish singing and make pictures of nature. Every chant and picture must be correct so that the girl would get well. I watched him and sighed. How would I ever learn all that I would need to know to become a medicine man myself someday?

T·H·I·N·K·I·N·G FOCUS

Why was sand painting important to the Navajo?

Key Terms

- chant
- sand painting

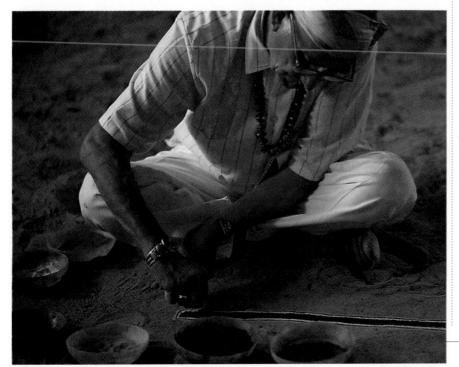

◄ *Today, Navajo medicine men still make sand paintings. This medicine man takes a pinch of color from one of the bowls and sprinkles it in a design to make a beautiful work of art.*

103

Close to Nature

The medicine man's young helper that you just read about believed that the chants and sand paintings had been given to the Navajo by the spirits of nature. **Sand paintings** are pictures made with bits of crushed rock, plants, and other dry materials. The paintings tell stories about nature and Navajo spirits.

The Navajo believed that, long ago, the spirits told them to paint pictures on the ground with colors of the earth. The spirits warned the Navajo not to save the paintings because people might fight to get them. So the Navajo made sand paintings on the earth floors of their hogans and swept them up after 12 hours. In that time, the power of the painting would have helped those who needed it.

▼ *Here is a finished sand painting. It shows the four Wind People spirits. Each spirit rules the wind from one of the four directions of the earth. In one hand they hold clouds, in the other they hold a feather used to make the winds blow.*

The Navajo first learned sand painting from other Indians who lived nearby. But in Navajo myths, the Wind People taught the Navajo how to make sand paintings. The Wind People are the spirits of nature whom you just saw in the sand painting on page 104.

The Navajo believed that living happily with the land, the air, and all living things was the only way to stay healthy. If someone got sick, they thought that using the art of the Wind People in ceremonies would make the person well.

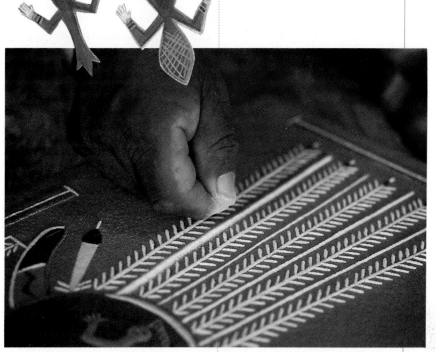

◄ *Sand paintings show just about anything in nature. Here, for example, is an otter and a beaver from a sand painting.*

▲ *The Navajo used 500 different sand paintings. A medicine man had to remember each line, since pictures of the paintings were not kept in any book.*

A ceremony to help someone get well often included many chants and several sand paintings. A medicine man would sing the chants and create the paintings. Each painting told a story about people and spirits in Navajo myth. The Navajo believed that when a sick person sat inside the painting, its power would help that person get well. ■

■ *How did the Navajo use sand paintings?*

A Story to Tell

The Navajo wondered how and why things in nature came to be. Why do big rocks exist? Where do mountains come from? What makes the wind blow and the rain fall? The Navajo told myths to answer these questions.

In myths, things in nature often became spirits who explained why things happened. For example, real rainbows in the sky became the Rainbow People in stories and sand paintings. Let's look at a sand painting of the Rainbow People and the story it tells about nature.

Reading a Sand Painting

This Rainbow People sand painting tells part of a Navajo myth that explains that water is a source of life. The circle in the center of the sand painting is a symbol for the source of all water on earth.

Look at the colors! The Navajo use white to show east, black for north, blue for south, and yellow for west. These colors come from crushed rocks and plants.

Navajo spirits with long bodies are shown on most sand paintings. The spirits in this painting are Rainbow People. They are wearing tall hats topped with feathers.

To protect the painting's power, another rainbow spirit wraps her extra-long body around three sides of the sand painting. Most sand paintings have protection bands like this.

Why do you think the Navajo told myths about the Rainbow People? Suppose you lived in a hot, dry desert. What would your most important resource be? If you said "water," you would be right. That's why you would always be happy to see a rainbow. It is a sign that rain has come.

Rainbow People were often used to protect three sides of sand paintings. That is because the Navajo felt safe when they saw a rainbow. It was a sign that life-giving rain had brought water to their crops.

◄ *The Navajo used tools like these to grind up rocks and plants to make the colors for their sand paintings. Many of the colors came from the colorful cliffs where they lived.*

Look at the Rainbow People sand painting on page 106. You can see four plants watered by rain. Beans, squash, tobacco, and corn grow between the pairs of Rainbow People. In the center box of the sand painting are symbols for clouds, water, and sunshine. Water and sunshine bring life to the earth because they help plants grow. Water and sunshine also create real rainbows in the sky. That is how this sand painting, and the story it tells, celebrate the beauty of nature. ■

◄ *Jet, which is a type of coal found in the Southwest, was often used for the color black in Navajo sand paintings.*

■ *Describe some of the things the Rainbow People sand painting tells us about nature.*

R E V I E W

1. **FOCUS** Why was sand painting important to the Navajo?
2. **CONNECT** Compare the way the Navajo saw nature with the way the Cheyenne saw nature. How are they alike?
3. **CRITICAL THINKING** What skills did a medicine man need to create sand paintings?
4. **ACTIVITY** Draw a picture of a sand painting you would like to make. You might include something from the sky or from the earth, such as the moon, lightning, animals, people, trees, or a river. Make up a story that your sand painting tells.

Using Scale

Here's Why You can use a map to help you get from one place to another. The scale on a map will help you figure out how far it is from one place to another.

Here's How Maps are drawn to scale. A scale is a way to show how far apart things are on the real earth. A certain distance on the map is equal to a larger distance on the real earth. Look at the map of the area around Bright Star's village on the next page. Find the scale. It shows that one inch on the map stands for one mile in real distance.

Now take your ruler and measure the distance between Bright Star's village and the place marked A on the stream. The two places are about two inches apart on the map. So, they are about two miles apart in real distance.

Measure the distance between Bright Star's village and the place marked B on the cliffs. About how far apart are the two places on the map? About how far apart are they in real distance? Bright Star can walk one mile in one-half hour. How long will it take her to walk from her village to place B on the cliffs?

Measure the distance between A and B on the map. About how far apart are the two places on the map? How many miles is that in real distance?

Try It Measure the distance between other points on the map. About how far away from each other are they in real distance? Use your ruler and the map scale to find out.

Sheep pasture

A
● Stream

E ●
Sage

B
● Cliffs

●
Bright Star's
village

D
● Corn field

Scale

1 inch = 1 mile

Apply It Work with a group to make a scale drawing
of your classroom. You will need a measuring tape and
a large piece of drawing paper. Use the measuring tape
to measure the length of each wall. Draw a scale outline
of the room on the drawing paper. One inch on your
outline should stand for one foot of real distance in
your classroom.

Then draw shapes to stand for large objects in your
classroom, such as students' desks, teacher's desk, and
bookcases. Try to put the objects in your drawing about
where they are in your classroom.

109

Chapter Review

Reviewing Key Terms

adaptation (p. 101) livestock (p. 100)
chant (p. 103) sand painting (p. 104)
hogan (p. 99)

A. Write the key term for each meaning.

1. a song sung on a few notes, often as a prayer
2. a one-room Navajo house
3. a picture made of crushed rock, plants, and other dried materials
4. animals raised to be used or sold
5. a change in the way of life to fit the surroundings

B. Write one or two sentences telling why each of the following sentences is true.

1. A hogan was a very good house for desert living.
2. Raising livestock was important to the Navajo.
3. A Navajo chant was a kind of medicine.

Exploring Concepts

A. Copy the chart below. Fill in the second column to show how the Kwakiutl and the Navajo were alike. Fill in the third column to show how the Kwakiutl and the Navajo were different.

B. Write one or two sentences to answer each question.

1. How did the Navajo adapt to the desert?
2. How did the Navajo use their sand paintings?

Indian people	How they were alike	How they were different
Kwakiutl and Navajo		

Reviewing Skills

A. Use a ruler and the map on the right.

1. About how many miles is it from Sam's house to the school? Use Second Street.
2. About how many miles is it from the school to the library? Use both Maryland Avenue and Third Street.

B. Write a sentence that tells what direction Sam's house is from the library.

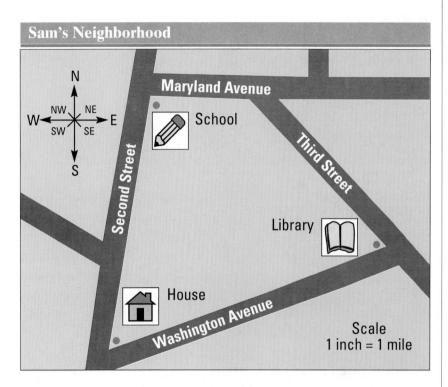

Sam's Neighborhood

N
NW   NE
W   E
SW   SE
S

Maryland Avenue

Second Street

Third Street

School

Library

House

Washington Avenue

Scale
1 inch = 1 mile

Using Critical Thinking

1. The Navajo learned from their neighbors how to raise livestock and crops. If they had not learned, how would their life have been different?

2. The Navajo made blankets and clothing from wool. Why do you think they used wool?

Preparing for Citizenship

1. **WRITING ACTIVITY** Pretend you live in a Navajo hogan with your family long ago. Write a story about one day in your life. Use your imagination, but include some of the facts about Navajo life that you have learned. Read your story to your class. Listen while other students read their stories. Put all of your stories together into one class book.

2. **COLLABORATIVE LEARNING** Make a mural of a sand painting. First, class members can decide what pictures to include. Some class members can draw the design. Other class members can paint. Choose one person to tell about your sand painting to another class in your school.

Unit 3

Settling the Land

American Indians lived on the land for thousands of years before settlers arrived from Europe. The settlers first built homes along the northeastern coast. As more people arrived, cities sprang up all along the Atlantic coast. Settlers looking for more space moved west. They traveled through thick forests, climbed great mountains, and crossed prairies and deserts on trails leading west. Some people went as far as the Pacific Ocean. Whether they were crossing the ocean or following trails to the Pacific, early settlers hoped that at the end of their journey they would find land to call their own.

Moses Speese Family. Custer County, Nebraska. 1888.
Solomon D. Butcher Collection. Nebraska State Historical Society.

Chapter 7

Settling the Northeast

In 1620, the Pilgrims started out on a long journey from England and landed on the northeast coast of North America. Indians helped the Pilgrims learn how to adapt to the land. As more settlers came and cities grew, people moved away from the coast and cleared land for homes and farms in eastern forests.

Before Pilgrims settled in Plymouth, they landed near Cape Cod. The only other English settlement then was in Virginia.

Thanksgiving with Indians is an unfinished painting from the 1940s by N. C. Wyeth. It shows Pilgrims sharing their first harvest with their Indian friends.

This farmhouse was built in 1720 by settlers in eastern Pennsylvania. By that time, many farmers lived in the woods of the Northeast.

By the middle 1700s, many people had settled west of the coastal cities. Farmers used plows like this to turn tree-covered areas into farmland.

Life in Plymouth

What challenges did the Pilgrims face during their first year in the new homeland?

Key Terms

- colony
- survive

Pretend you are living long ago in England. Your family has decided to make a new home far away, so you leave your home and friends. For 65 days you sail across the ocean. All the way, you wonder about your new home. Will it be cozy? Will the English people who moved there first be friendly? Will they have children your own age?

Tired from the stormy journey, you finally spot land. You search the coast for the neighbors you expected, but there is no sign of them. You can't keep looking. It is getting colder and you must choose a place to stay. As you wade to shore, no one greets you. No one offers you a hot meal or a warm bed. With only a few belongings, you must start a new life in a cold, strange land.

➤ Landing of the Pilgrims *was painted in the early 1800s. Pilgrims did row ashore in small boats, but the painting is incorrect in showing the Indians waiting on shore. The Pilgrims didn't meet the Indians until the following spring.*

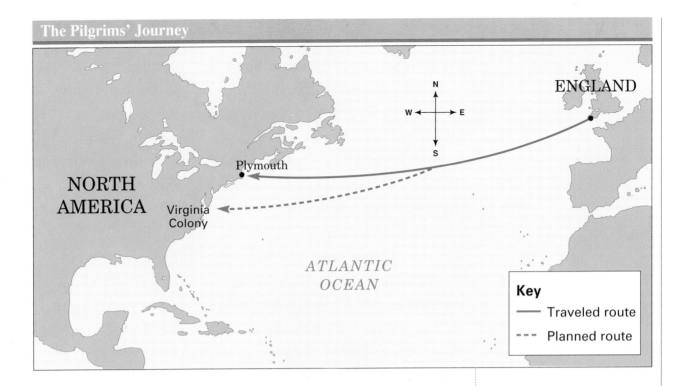

ENGLAND

NORTH
AMERICA

Plymouth

Virginia
Colony

ATLANTIC
OCEAN

Key

—— Traveled route

- - - Planned route

The Pilgrims' First Winter

That's how many Pilgrims felt who sailed from England on a ship called the *Mayflower* in the summer of 1620. The Pilgrims were a religious group who disagreed with the church in England. They decided to raise their children in a whole new place.

The Pilgrims had planned to join a colony already started in Virginia. A **colony** is a settlement ruled by a distant country. However, the *Mayflower* did not follow the route to Virginia. Instead, it landed in late November on what is now the coast of Massachusetts.

Not finding the neighbors they expected, the Pilgrims looked for a place to begin their own colony. Four weeks later, in late December, they chose a spot and named it Plymouth after a town in England. Notice how far Virginia Colony is from Plymouth on the map above.

Plymouth was rich in natural resources. It had good farmland and many streams. Forests were a source for wood and animal meat. From the sea they got lobster, clams, and fish. Still, the Pilgrims barely **survived,** or lived through, that first winter. They had not brought enough extra food with them to last until spring, and there were

Across Time & Space

Historians are not sure what happened to the Mayflower *after the crew returned it to England in the spring of 1621. Some believe that an English farmer bought the* Mayflower *and used part of it as a barn roof. The barn still stands in a village outside London.*

few animals around to be hunted in the wintertime.

During their voyage, the Pilgrims had not eaten any fresh foods. The winter cold destroyed any green vegetables and berries that grew in Plymouth. Without these foods, many Pilgrims got sick. Two or three people died almost every week. To add to their worries, the Pilgrims didn't know if the Indians who lived nearby were going to be friendly.

To make matters even worse, the Pilgrims settled in Plymouth at the beginning of the cold New England winter. They needed to find shelter right away. All winter, the women stayed on board the *Mayflower* to take care of the children. The men rowed ashore to hunt, living in caves or holes dug into the sides of hills. They built rough roofs and doorways out of logs and mud mixed with stones and sticks. These shelters were all that protected the men from the icy weather. ■

■ Find facts to support this statement: The first winter the Pilgrims spent in America was very difficult.

Help from the Wampanoag

When spring finally arrived, only half of the 102 people that sailed from England were still alive. Women and children who had survived the winter joined the others on shore. The Pilgrims were determined to build a new English colony at Plymouth. Soon after, the Pilgrims met their Indian neighbors, the Wampanoag *(wahm puh NOH uhg)*.

Without help from the Wampanoag, the Pilgrims may never have been able to survive another winter. They taught the Pilgrims how to grow beans and pumpkins, and corn like that shown here. They also showed the Pilgrims that burying fish makes the soil richer for growing crops. The Wampanoag taught the colonists where and how to hunt and catch fish. The Pilgrims no longer feared that these people might be unfriendly. In fact, the Wampanoag proved to be great friends.

Thanks to the Wampanoag and lots of hard work, the Pilgrims adapted to their new land. That fall, they had a plentiful harvest. The Pilgrims were able to store enough food to last through the winter. They held a feast to give thanks to God. They invited the Wampanoag to share the foods the Wampanoag had made possible. This feast was the first Thanksgiving. ■

■ *How did the Wampanoag help the Pilgrims?*

First Year in Plymouth, From Fall to Fall

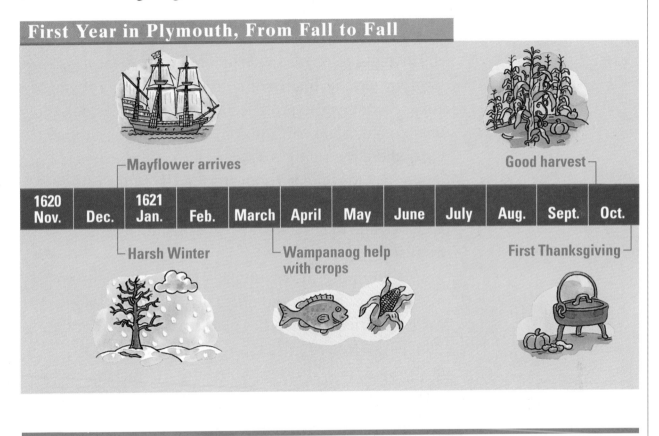

Mayflower arrives

Good harvest

1620 Nov.	Dec.	1621 Jan.	Feb.	March	April	May	June	July	Aug.	Sept.	Oct.

Harsh Winter

Wampanaog help with crops

First Thanksgiving

R E V I E W

1. **FOCUS** What challenges did the Pilgrims face during their first year in the new homeland?

2. **CONNECT** Compare the materials the Navajo used to build hogans with the materials the Pilgrims used to build shelters that first year at Plymouth.

3. **CRITICAL THINKING** How did the Pilgrims' arrival in winter make their first few months harder than if they had arrived in the spring?

4. **ACTIVITY** Look at the timeline on this page. It shows the Pilgrims' first year at Plymouth. Think about a typical year in your own life. When do you start school? When do you celebrate the New Year? When is your birthday? Make up a timeline for yourself. Draw pictures to show what events you celebrate.

Why Countries Had Colonies

When the Pilgrims began the Plymouth settlement, they were not planning to start a new country with new rulers. Instead, they claimed the land as a part of England. The Pilgrims remained citizens of England, and they were still ruled by English laws. Settlements like theirs, ruled by a country far away, are called colonies.

Having a colony helped a country in several ways. A colony gave its home country new lands for growing crops. A colony also provided natural resources, such as timber, gold, silver, oil, and coal. A colony was another place where the ruling country could sell its products. Finally, a colony made products that the ruling country could sell to other countries. Countries that had colonies often became richer and more powerful than other countries.

England was just one of many countries that ruled over colonies. France and Spain also had colonies in North America and in other places. Today, most of the colonies are free countries.

Life in the Eastern Forest

Adim lantern glow lit up the log cabin. It was 8:00 P.M., time for Maddie to go to bed. Pulling her nightcap down over her ears, she crawled in beside her sleeping sister. The wooden planks of the bed creaked. Each time Maddie moved, the dry leaves and cornhusks crackled inside the bed padding. During the summer, the deerhide covers felt itchy, and there were often bedbugs in it. But on this cold winter night, the bed felt cozy. Maddie snuggled under the hide, listened for a moment to the trees howling in the wind, then fell fast asleep.

THINKING
FOCUS

What was life like for the people who moved from the coastal cities into the wilderness?

Key Terms

- inland
- goods
- wilderness

Moving Inland

Soon after the Pilgrims and other early settlers came to this country, cities began to grow along the Atlantic coast. By the early 1700s, there were several big cities with many people. People began to move **inland,** or away from the coast. Many families like Maddie's moved into the Pennsylvania forests. There they would build a log cabin and rough cornhusk beds and start farming.

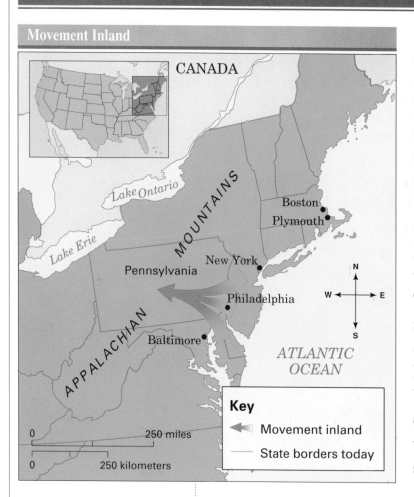

CANADA

Lake Ontario

Lake Erie

MOUNTAINS

APPALACHIAN

Boston

Plymouth

New York

Pennsylvania

Philadelphia

Baltimore

ATLANTIC OCEAN

N
W E
S

Key

Movement inland

State borders today

0   250 miles

0   250 kilometers

Many of these settlers came from Germany, Ireland, and Scotland. They moved to Pennsylvania for many reasons. Some, like Maddie's family, wanted to own their own land.

These farmers grew food to sell to the big eastern cities like Philadelphia. These cities were growing very quickly. The people in them needed more **goods,** or supplies, in order to live. Find Philadelphia on the map. What are some of the other cities near the Atlantic coast where farmers might have sold their food?

Trappers and hunters also moved inland. They provided city people with goods from the forest. Forest goods included animal hides and furs, and special plants called herbs. Colonists used hides and furs for clothing and blankets. They used herbs to make medicines. ■

■ *What were some of the reasons settlers moved inland?*

Clearing the Land

Land west of Philadelphia was mostly wilderness. A **wilderness** is land that has not been changed by farms or buildings. Indians living in these forests had built villages and cleared some land for crops. However, most of the land was still covered by thick forests.

Farmers needed open space to build homes and plant crops. When they found a flat place near fresh water, they cleared the wilderness by cutting down trees. Then they built cabins from logs from the trees. Settlers needed a one-room log cabin and a corn crop to survive the winter.

How Do We Know?

Wilderness settlers were very busy, but they still found time to write. They wrote letters to friends and sometimes kept diaries. These writings help us know what life was like for those settlers.

Settlers could not survive without two important tools—an ax and rifle. They used axes to clear land, chop firewood, and cut logs for the cabin. Settlers used rifles to kill deer, bears, squirrels, and turkey. Without rifles, settlers would not have eaten much meat. ■

■ *Why were axes and rifles so important to settlers in the wilderness?*

Everyday Life

To survive, settlers had to make almost everything they needed themselves. In cities, people could buy goods from stores. There were no stores deep in the wilderness.

Wood was the most important resource in the settlers' everyday lives. Settlers used wood to build their cabins, and nearly everything that went inside. They used wood to make wagons, tools, cradles, benches, and bowls.

Wilderness settlers often lived far apart, but they would gather from miles around to help a new neighbor raise logs for a new cabin. Settlers turned these "log raisings" into a chance to visit. You'll read more about building a log cabin on the next page.

◄ *This settler is cooking supper in her fireplace. How many things can you see in her cabin that are made of wood?*

A Log Raising

Think about your home. Can you imagine building it? What a job! To build their houses, settlers used axes to cut down trees and to make the logs fit together.

U-shaped cuts were chopped into the ends of the logs. The cuts helped the logs fit together.

Helping hands from neighbors made the four main steps in building a log cabin go quickly.
1. Logs were dragged to the spot where the cabin would be built.
2. Bottom logs were put in place.
3. Ropes were used to pull wall logs up poles.
4. Roof and chimney were put up.

Mud, moss, and stones were mixed to fill the chinks, or holes, between the logs.

◄ In this 1796 sketch, a settler takes a break from her chores to look at her surroundings.

▼ Sometimes settlers used axes to plant seeds if they didn't have proper farming tools.

After all the hard work of putting up a cabin, settlers enjoyed music, feasting, and storytelling. A finished log cabin might have looked like the one above.

Like the Pilgrims, the Pennsylvania settlers learned many of the skills they needed from their Indian neighbors. In the Pennsylvania forests, these were the Delaware Indians.

Like the Wampanoag, the Delaware knew how to use the natural resources of the land. The Delaware taught the settlers how to grow corn, beans, and squash. The Indians even shared recipes for cooking these foods. The Delaware also showed the settlers which wild herbs made the best medicines. ■

■ *How did the settlers adapt to the land?*

R E V I E W

1. **FOCUS** What was life like for the people who moved from the coastal cities into the wilderness?

2. **CONNECT** Compare the way settlers and the Kwakiutl depended on forest goods.

3. **CRITICAL THINKING** Explain how you would feel about moving to the wilderness.

4. **ACTIVITY** Pretend you are a new settler traveling through the wilderness. Write a short description of what you are carrying and how you find food and shelter each day.

"If . . . Then" Statements

Here's Why You have learned that many settlers moved inland to the wilderness. They must have thought carefully about the move before they made it. They may have thought of many reasons to move and many reasons not to move. They could have used "If . . . then" statements to help them decide.

Here's How An "If . . . then" statement is a way of thinking about or talking about the results of doing something. Some results may be good. Some may not be so good.

For example, suppose a family were thinking of moving to the wilderness. Here are two possible results:

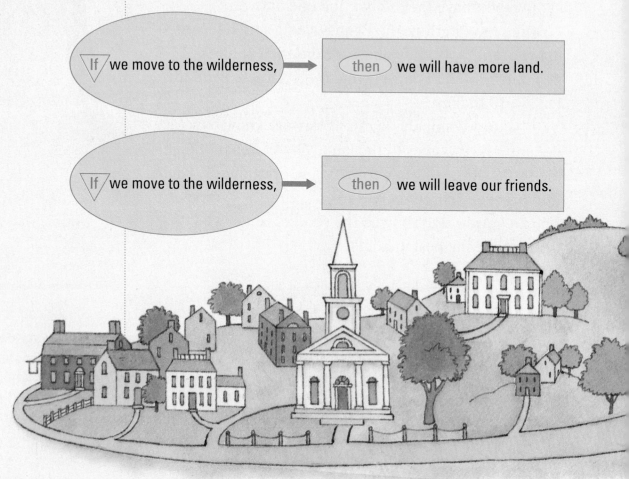

If we move to the wilderness, → then we will have more land.

If we move to the wilderness, → then we will leave our friends.

Perhaps some families moved because having more land was more important than living near old friends. Why do you think some families decided not to move?

"If . . . then" statements can help us make a decision. They help us see that most things we do have results.

Try It   Think of two other possible results of a family's move to the wilderness. Write each result as an "If . . . then" statement. Share your statements with your class.

Apply It   Suppose your family is thinking of getting a new puppy. Think of some possible results. Then write "If . . . then" statements that tell what might happen.

Early Settlers

Pretend you are a detective. You have been asked to discover who started your community and what it was like long ago. How would you get this information?

Get Ready   Every detective looks for clues to find information. You can find clues about the beginning of your community by looking at the names of streets and buildings. Some of them are named for people who started your community.

Find Out   Look through books to find out more about these early settlers. You can also find old pictures or photographs in books. You may even find old maps of your community.

La Clede Landing at Present site of St. Louis

Move Ahead   Write a report on what you discovered about the people who started your community and about its early years. Draw some pictures to go with your report.

Explore Some More   Make a class scrapbook of the early years of your community. Put your written report and pictures in the scrapbook. Include a list of streets and buildings that were named for people who started your community. Add any pictures and maps from the past that you can find. You may want to give your class scrapbook to your school or community library.

Joseph Morgan founded Morgantown in 1949

This is when he was a baby. He was born in 1904.

He grew up above his father's dry goods store in Pottersville.

his grandparents

He married Ch...

Chapter Review

Reviewing Key Terms

colony (p. 117) survive (p. 117)
goods (p. 122) wilderness (p. 122)
inland (p. 121)

A. Write the key term that best completes each sentence.

1. During their first winter, the Pilgrims were barely able to _____.
2. A _____ is land that has not been changed by people.
3. A settlement ruled by a country far away is called a _____.
4. People buy _____, or supplies.
5. We move _____ when we move away from the coast.

B. Write *true* or *false* for each sentence below. If a sentence is false, rewrite it to make it true.

1. The Wampanoag helped the Pilgrims survive their second winter in Plymouth.
2. Hunters and farmers sold goods to people in cities.
3. In the colonies, the settlers had an easy life.
4. A colony belongs to another country.
5. Wilderness families lived far apart from one another.

Exploring Concepts

A. The Pilgrims and the Navajo learned from other people. Copy the chart below and fill in the last two columns. Your chart will show what the Pilgrims and the Navajo learned and from whom they learned.

B. Answer the questions in one or two sentences.

1. Why were colonies important to their home countries?
2. Why did people move to the wilderness where life was hard?

People	What they learned	From whom
The Navajo		
The Pilgrims		

Reviewing Skills

1. Write two "If . . . then" statements to tell what might happen if you move to a new city.
2. What physical features are shown on the map at the right?
3. Look at the map on the right again. What direction is Philadelphia from New York City? Is the distance between the two cities less than or more than 250 miles?

Lake Ontario

Lake Erie

MOUNTAINS

Boston
Plymouth

New York

Pennsylvania

Philadelphia

APPALACHIAN

Baltimore

ATLANTIC
OCEAN

N
W — E
S

Key

Movement inland

State borders today

0   250 miles

0   250 kilometers

Using Critical Thinking

1. If the Pilgrims had arrived at a desert in the summer, would more people have survived the first six months? Why?
2. When settlers in the forests built their own homes, other people came to help. What can we do today to help people who have no homes?
3. Rifles and axes were important tools for settlers. What are our most important tools today?

Preparing for Citizenship

1. **WRITING ACTIVITY** Pretend you are a settler in the wilderness. Write a letter to a friend in England. Tell what you usually do during the day.
2. **COLLABORATIVE LEARNING** Work with other students in a group. Choose an event in the lives of the Pilgrims or the Pennsylvania settlers. Help your group act out your event for the rest of the class. The landing of the Pilgrims at Plymouth is one event that you could act out. A log raising by the settlers is another. After your group is finished, the rest of the class should try to guess the event you acted out. Try to guess the events acted out by other groups.

131

Chapter 8

Beyond the Appalachians

As more and more cities grew in the East, many settlers packed all that they owned to journey to new land in the West. First, they had to cross the Appalachian (ap uh LAY chee uhn) Mountains to settle in Kentucky. Later, wagons followed trails that led as far west as Oregon and California. It took about a hundred years, from the end of the 1700s to the end of the 1800s, to settle the West. During this time, the West became a land of growth and change.

This child's cradle was made during the middle 1800s. Babies born along the western trails slept in cradles like this.

Oscar Berninghaus painted *Oregon Trail* in 1951. It shows families making the long trip across the United States.

Some settlers' children attended schools like this one in Kansas. Children of all ages were taught by the same teacher. This one-room schoolhouse was made of big blocks of grass-covered earth.

Here are some of the hunting tools that people took with them on their trip west. The bag held bullets and other hunting materials. In the large horn was powder that would make the rifle fire. The pick and the brush were used to clean the gun, and the tiny horn was used to measure powder.

133

The Wilderness Road

Key Terms

- pioneer
- blaze

➤ *The Cumberland Gap is a natural passageway through the Appalachian Mountains. Thousands of settlers traveled through this gap on their way to Kentucky.*

> *S*atrd April 8th—We all pact up and started crost Cumberland gap about one oclock this Day We Met a great maney peopel turned Back for fear of the indians but our Company goes on Still with good courage we come to a very ugly Creek with steep Banks and have it to cross several times. . . .
>
> William Calk, from his journal, 1775

William Calk may not have spelled very well, but he had many adventures along the Wilderness Road. Despite the dangers of travel, Calk was determined to reach Kentucky. It was a beautiful land with lots of open space.

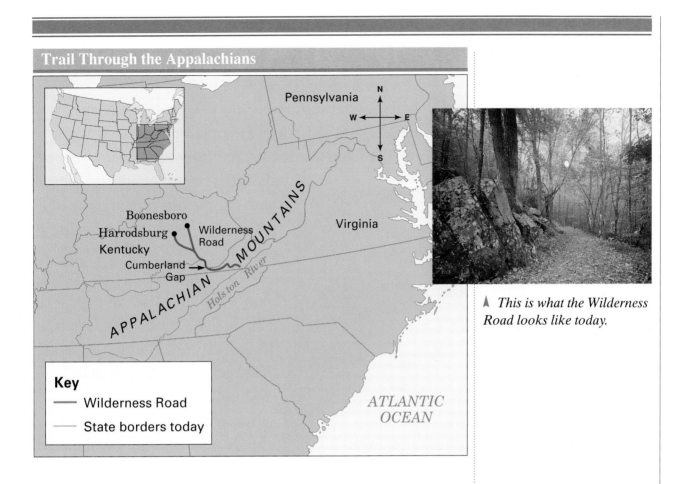

▲ *This is what the Wilderness Road looks like today.*

A Difficult Crossing

William Calk was a **pioneer,** which is a person who leaves a settled place and moves into the wilderness to make a new home. In the late 1700s and early 1800s, thousands of pioneers like Calk moved to Kentucky. Why did they move to Kentucky? For one thing, land cost less there than along the east coast. For another, Kentucky had rich soil for farming. Herds of buffalo and other wild animals roamed there. People said there were so many birds in Kentucky that they could block out the sun.

Kentucky offered much, but getting there was difficult and dangerous. Notice on the map how the Appalachian Mountains blocked all travel west. If people wanted to reach Kentucky, they first had to haul everything they owned over these rugged mountains.

Narrow Indian or buffalo paths crossed some of these mountains. Pioneers had to follow these paths on foot or by horse. The paths were far too narrow for wagons. ■

■ *Why did the Appalachian Mountains present problems to pioneers who wanted to move west?*

135

Daniel Boone Leads the Way

▼ *Many believe that this piece of tree bark was carved by Daniel Boone in his travels through the Appalachians. It is dated 1775.*

■ *How did Daniel Boone help settle the land west of the Appalachian Mountains?*

To help people settle in Kentucky, pioneers needed a better way to get there. Some people bought Kentucky land from the Cherokee *(CHAIR uh kee)* Indians in order to sell it to new settlers. Then these same people hired Daniel Boone to **blaze,** or mark, a trail for the settlers.

To build the Wilderness Road, Daniel Boone gathered a crew of 30 men. Their job was to clear the way from Virginia to Kentucky. The crew had to widen the trails that were already there. Sometimes they made new trails and connected them to the old ones.

Boone led the way, blazing trees to mark the route of the trail. His crew followed, clearing away underbrush and chopping down trees. Look at the map on page 135 again. Trace the Wilderness Road from the Holston River to the Cumberland Gap. At which two Kentucky towns did parts of the road end? ■

Traveling the Wilderness Road

In 1774, Boone's Wilderness Road was finally ready. The road made travel easier, but it was still a difficult trip. Pioneers had to carry everything on horseback or in wagons. Storms caused serious delays. Flooded streams and rivers were hard to cross. Wagon wheels often got stuck in the mud after a heavy rain. Repairing broken wagons was difficult because pioneers had few tools or parts.

Sometimes pioneers were turned back by Cherokee attacks. Kentucky had been Cherokee hunting ground for hundreds of years. The Cherokee had sold part of the land, but people were settling in places that had never been sold. Also, there were more settlers than the Cherokee had expected. The Cherokee were being forced to live in lands farther to the west. Their people were losing the ways that they had lived for hundreds of years.

Until 1818, when other roads opened up for use, thousands of settlers used the Wilderness Road. Many of these first pioneers were the children and grandchildren of the German and other pioneer families who had settled the eastern Pennsylvania forest years before. ■

■ *What made a trip on the Wilderness Road so difficult?*

◄ *This sketch of a pioneer family crossing the Appalachians was drawn by someone who was actually there, Joshua Shaw.*

R E V I E W

1. **FOCUS** Why was the Wilderness Road important to the people who wanted to settle in Kentucky?
2. **CONNECT** Compare problems that Plymouth colonists had with problems that Kentucky pioneers had. What were some of the differences?
3. **CRITICAL THINKING** If you were a Cherokee, how might you feel about settlers moving into your hunting grounds?
4. **WRITING ACTIVITY** Write a journal entry for a day on the Wilderness Road. You have to cross several deep streams with steep banks with your wagon and horses. Describe what you did to get across.

Many years ago, men, women, and children—young and old alike—went west to find a new land to settle. Travel was not easy. Houses and food were hard to find. But, always, other people helped. Read this excerpt from a story about a pioneer family in Kansas.

LITERATURE

WAGON WHEELS

Written by Barbara Brenner

Illustrated by Don Bolognese

Chapter 1—THE DUGOUT

There it is, boys," Daddy said. "Across this river is Nicodemus, Kansas. That is where we are going to build our house. There is free land for everyone here in the West. All we have to do is go and get it."

We had come a long way to get to Kansas. All the way from Kentucky. It had been a hard trip, and a sad one. Mama died on the way. Now there were just the four of us—Daddy, Willie, Little Brother, and me. "Come on, boys," Daddy called. "Let's put our feet on free dirt." We crossed the river, wagon and all.

A man was waiting for us on the other side.
"I am Sam Hickman," he said. "Welcome to the
town of Nicodemus."

"Why, thank you, Brother," Daddy said.
"But where *is* your town?"

"Right here," Mr. Hickman said. We did not
see any houses. But we saw smoke coming out
of holes in the prairie.

"Shucks!" my Daddy said. "Holes in the
ground are for rabbits and snakes, not for free
black people. I am a carpenter. I can build fine
wood houses for this town."

"No time to build wood houses now," Mr.
Hickman told my Daddy. "Winter is coming.
And winter in Kansas is *mean*. Better get
yourself a dugout before the ground freezes."
Daddy knew Sam Hickman was right. We got
our shovels and we dug us a dugout.

It wasn't much of a place—dirt floor, dirt
walls, no windows. And the roof was just
grass and branches. But we were glad to have
that dugout when the wind began to whistle
across the prairie.

Every night Willie lit the lamp and made a fire. I cooked a rabbit stew or fried a pan of fish fresh from the river. After supper Daddy would always say, "How about a song or two?" He would take out his banjo and *Plink-a-plunk! Plink-a-plunk!* Pretty soon that dugout felt like home.

Chapter II—INDIANS

Winter came. And that Kansas winter *was* mean. It snowed day after day. We could not hunt or fish. We had no more rabbit stew. No more fish fresh from the river. All we had was cornmeal mush to eat.

Then one day there was no more cornmeal. There was not a lick of food in the whole town of Nicodemus. And nothing left to burn for firewood. Little Brother cried all the time—he was so cold and hungry. Daddy wrapped blankets around him. "Hush, baby son," he said to him. "Try to sleep. Supply train will be coming soon." But the supply train did not come. Not that day or the next.

On the third day we heard the sound of horses. Daddy looked out to see who it was. "Oh Lord!" he said. "Indians!" We were *so* scared. We had all heard stories about Indians. I tried to be brave.

"I will get my gun, Daddy," I said.

But Daddy said, "Hold on, Johnny. Wait and see what they do." We watched from the dugout.

Everyone in Nicodemus was watching the Indians. First they made a circle. Then each Indian took something from his saddlebag and dropped it on the ground. The Indians turned and rode straight toward the dugouts. "Now they are coming for us!" Willie cried.

We raised our guns. But the Indians rode right past us and kept on going. We waited a long time to be sure they were gone. Then everyone ran out into the snow to see what the Indians had left. It was FOOD! Everyone talked at once. "Look!" "Fresh deer meat!" "Fish!" "Dried beans and squash!" "And bundles of sticks to keep our fires burning."

There was a feast in Nicodemus that night.
But before we ate, Daddy said to us, "Johnny.
Willie. Little Brother. I want you to remember
this day. When someone says bad things about
Indians, tell them the Osage Indians saved our
lives in Nicodemus."

Passages to the West

THINKING
FOCUS

Why did people travel on the Oregon Trail and the Santa Fe Trail?

Key Terms

- pass
- wagon train

Reggie walks along the trail in Scotts Bluff National Monument in western Nebraska. He tries to imagine the thousands of wagons that traveled this trail over a hundred years ago. He thinks about how excited the pioneers must have been when they reached Scotts Bluff.

The pioneers spent weeks crossing the Great Plains. The grassy land looked the same mile after mile. The pioneers could not tell how far they had come or how far they had to go. Scotts Bluff was the first sign these tired travelers had that their long prairie crossing was nearing an end. It also meant that their trip through the Rocky Mountains was about to begin.

Heading West

Since the early days of the colonies, Americans had been moving west. First, they moved into places like western Pennsylvania. Then they moved farther west into Kentucky and Missouri. The trail that Reggie saw was made by settlers moving as far west as Oregon. Many of these pioneers were the children, grandchildren, and great-grandchildren of the earlier pioneers.

Many pioneers went west to get away from crowded areas of the East or to start farms on cheap land in the West. Others went west to become miners. Miners are people who dig for gold, silver, and other valuable materials. Still others went west to buy and sell goods.

▼ *Fast-moving water and rocks and holes along river bottoms made river crossings dangerous for pioneers.*

The trip from the East to the far West was difficult. First, pioneers had to cross the Great Plains. This huge grassland lay empty and flat for hundreds of miles. Finding food and drinking water was often a problem. Some of the rivers they had to cross were dangerous.

Pioneers going to the Pacific coast had to cross high mountains. These were steep and sometimes covered with snow. Those going to the Southwest had to travel through a desert where there was little food or water. ■

■ *What were some of the reasons that pioneers traveled west, and why was the trip so difficult?*

The Sante Fe Trail

There were several trails that people could use to go west. Most travelers used either the Santa Fe (*SAN tuh FAY*) Trail or the Oregon Trail.

The Santa Fe Trail, which opened in 1821, was 780 miles long. It began in Independence, Missouri, and crossed the Great Plains. Then, instead of going over the Rocky Mountains, the trail dipped southwest. It went through the Cimarron Desert and ended in Santa Fe, New Mexico. Later the trail also went from Santa Fe to Los Angeles, California. Trace the route of the Sante Fe Trail on the map on page 149.

Most travelers on the Santa Fe Trail were traders. They went west with cloth, farm tools, and other goods from the East. They sold these goods in the West, where they bought furs, gold, silver, and more. Then they returned to the East for more selling and buying. ■

■ *Why did traders travel the Sante Fe Trail?*

▼ *These wagons may have been fuller when they reached the mountains. As pioneers crossed mountains, they often had to dump items to make their wagons easier to pull.*

The Oregon Trail

Unlike the Santa Fe Trail, the Oregon Trail was used by families. Most of them were heading west to set up farms and build homes.

Look again at the map. Notice that the Oregon Trail also began in Independence, Missouri. From there it wound 2,000 miles toward the Northwest. It crossed the Great Plains and passed over the Rocky Mountains through the South Pass. Going through a **pass,** or a low point in the mountains, made the trip easier. After crossing through South Pass, travelers could continue to what is now Oregon.

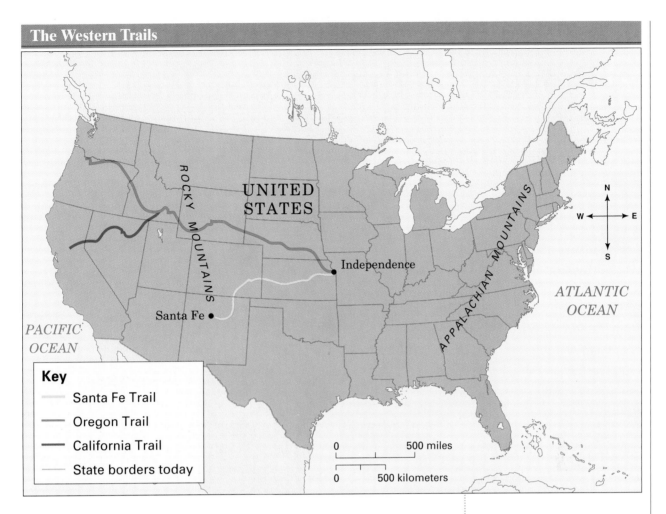

Key

— Santa Fe Trail

— Oregon Trail

— California Trail

— State borders today

UNITED STATES

ROCKY MOUNTAINS

APPALACHIAN MOUNTAINS

Independence

Santa Fe

PACIFIC OCEAN

ATLANTIC OCEAN

0   500 miles

0   500 kilometers

Some people on the Oregon Trail were heading to California. They hoped to find gold there. Those travelers could turn south from the Oregon Trail onto the California Trail.

Pioneer families traveled the Oregon Trail in **wagon trains.** As many as one hundred families would move along the trail in a long line of wagons pulled by oxen and mules. A scout, or guide, traveled with the wagon train. The scout knew where food, water, and good stopping places were.

Travelers on the Oregon Trail had to keep moving. It took four to six months to get to the end of the trail. They had to get through the Rocky Mountains before winter came, or snow and ice might trap them in the mountains. A wagon train usually moved no farther than 15 miles each day and stopped only at noon and at nightfall. Breakdowns or accidents might also force them to stop. The Moment in Time on the next page takes a look at a pioneer during one of these stops.

How Do We Know?

Pioneers on the Oregon Trail sometimes stopped at Independence Rock in Wyoming. Travelers would scratch their names in the rock there. We know this because their names are still there on the rock today.

A Pioneer on the Oregon Trail

4:50 P.M. May 7, 1843
On the banks of the Platte River
in central Nebraska

Firewood

Cottonwood branches make a great fire, and this woman plans to keep it going for several hours. After dinner, her new friends will join her family around the fire to talk about their plans to settle in Oregon.

Shawl

This woman's mother wore this colorful shawl when she traveled to America from Ireland. Now it is making another long journey as this pioneer crosses America.

Flint

Striking the rock in her pocket against a metal bar will make sparks to start a cooking fire. Tonight's dinner will be fresh fish from the Platte River.

Dress

Brand new at the start of the journey, this dress is now covered with prairie dust. The woman hopes that soon the wagon train will stop in one place long enough for her to wash it. The other dresses packed in her wagon are too fancy to wear on the trail.

Shoes

Before she left her farm in Ohio, this woman bought these tough leather shoes. The salesman who sold them to her said that they would hold up well on the rough, rocky trails of the mountains.

◄ *This is one of the few photographs taken of people on the Oregon Trail.*

▼ *This box holds medicine made from herbs. Pioneers brought medicine on the trail to help sick or injured travelers.*

The trip west on the Oregon Trail was difficult for travelers. Food, water, and firewood were hard to find along the trail. Sometimes Indians would help pioneers by giving them directions or trading with them. However, not all Indians were friendly. Some Indians felt that they were being forced off their land by the settlers. These Indians would sometimes attack a wagon train. Pioneers were also killed by accidents and sickness during their journey.

The days of pioneer travel were long and hard, but the wagon trains moved on. The pioneers looked forward to starting new lives in the West. ■

■ *What was life like on the Oregon Trail?*

R E V I E W

1. **FOCUS** Why did people travel on the Oregon Trail and the Santa Fe Trail?
2. **CONNECT** How was the journey of the Pilgrims on the *Mayflower* like the journey of the pioneers heading west on the trails? How was it different?
3. **CRITICAL THINKING** What do you think was one of the most difficult parts of a pioneer's life? What was the most exciting part? Explain.
4. **WRITING ACTIVITY** Imagine that you and a group of friends are going west a hundred years ago. You need to find a scout to guide your wagon train. Write a short paragraph that tells what kind of person you are looking for.

Packing Your Wagon for Oregon

Here's Why

Imagine that it is the year 1840. You and your family are going to move west. The trip will take four to six months. Everything you take will have to be packed in a covered wagon. You will have to pack some food and a few necessary items, such as pots and pans. The inside of the wagon is very small, about 16 feet long and 5 feet wide. What will you choose to take?

Here's How

Think about the things a pioneer family needed. Look at the items pictured on this page and on page 152 to get some ideas. What other things would you want to take in your wagon? Think about reasons for taking them.

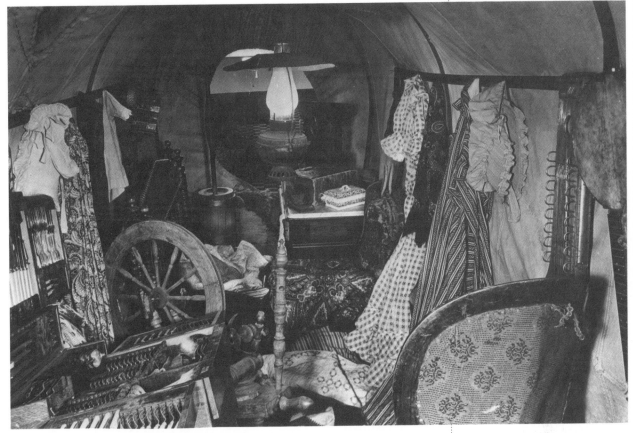

Try It

Work with a partner. Make a list of all the things you would like to pack in your wagon. List those things that you must take. Also, list things that would be nice to take if there is room for them.

Apply It

If you had room in your wagon for only five items, which five would you choose to take? Tell why you would take each one.

An Early Prairie Town

THINKING FOCUS

Why was Abilene known as a cattle town?

Key Terms

- population
- trade center

➤ *Nat Love was a famous cowboy who drove cattle across the prairies for nearly 20 years.*

Cowboys often sang as they moved cattle across the prairie. This song, "The Old Chisholm (*CHIHZ uhm*) Trail," was one of their favorites:

Oh come along, boys, and listen to my tale,
I'll tell you all my troubles on the ol' Chis'm trail.

Chorus: *Come a-ti yi youpy youpy ya youpy yay,*
Come a-ti yi youpy youpy yay.

On a ten-dollar horse and
a forty-dollar saddle,
I was ridin' and a-punchin'
Texas cattle.

(Chorus)

I'm up in the mornin'
afore daylight,
An' afore I sleep
the moon shines bright.

(Chorus)

It's bacon and beans
most every day,
I'd as soon be eatin'
prairie hay.

(Chorus)

Western Communities

Cowboys sang songs such as "The Old Chisholm Trail" to pass the time and to calm their herds. Cowboys were among the first people from the East to come to the prairies. But as the **population,** or number of people, in the United States grew in the 1860s, more and more people moved west.

The railroad brought many people to the prairies of Illinois, Missouri, and Kansas. Towns sprang up along the railroad line. Many people moved west to set up farms or to start businesses to serve the growing population already living there. The railroad also gave ranchers in the West a way to get cattle to markets in the East. ■

■ *Why did towns start springing up on the prairies?*

▲ *This picture shows Abilene, Kansas, during its peak as a cattle town.*

The Growth of Abilene

One of the fastest-growing prairie towns was Abilene, Kansas. The Chisholm Trail stretched from San Antonio, Texas, to Abilene. This was the main trail for driving cattle out of Texas during the late 1860s. The railroad was also very important to Abilene's growth. For a few years,

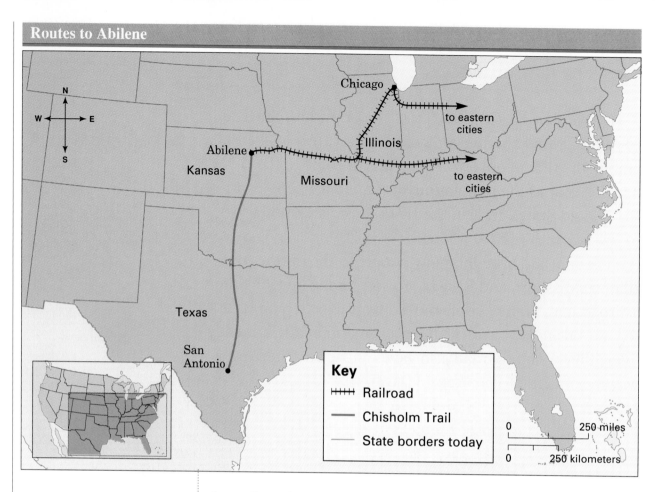

Key

┼┼┼┼ Railroad

───── Chisholm Trail

───── State borders today

0   250 miles

0   250 kilometers

Cowboys are now called cowhands. Life for many cowboys has changed. Today some cowhands use helicopters to look for missing cattle. They may move cattle from place to place in trucks.

■ *Why did Abilene grow so quickly?*

156

the railroad ended in Abilene. Abilene's location at the end of the Chisholm Trail and at the end of the railroad made it an important western town.

People in the East needed beef. Cowboys drove cattle from Texas north along the Chisholm Trail to Abilene. From there, cattle were loaded onto trains and shipped to Chicago where they were prepared to be sold as meat in the East. Use the map to trace the routes used to move cattle from San Antonio to eastern cities.

Visitors to Abilene one hundred years ago could see in a minute that it was a cattle town. Cowboys and cattle were everywhere! Cowboys, happy to be done with a long cattle drive, wandered the streets. Cattle rattled pens and clattered up loading ramps onto trains.

Many businesses moved to Abilene. It quickly grew from a small prairie town into a busy **trade center,** or place to do business. Farmers near the town sold food to the cowboys. Hotels, stores, and other businesses provided cowboys with places to eat, sleep, and buy goods. ■

The Cowboys Move On

In 1871, Abilene's Texas cattle business came to an end. People and businesses started leaving. Abilene was no longer a busy trade center. This graph shows the change in the number of cattle that passed through Abilene.

Abilene's cattle business stopped for many reasons. Some settlers around Abilene were unfriendly to the cowboys. Also, Texas cattle were no longer allowed into areas of Kansas near Abilene. They carried a sickness that made cattle raised on the northern plains very ill. Texas ranchers did not like this new law against their cattle.

The most important reason that Abilene lost cattle business was that new railroads were built. They led to cities that were closer to Texas where cattle were raised than Abilene was. Cowboys no longer had to drive cattle as far as Abilene to reach railroad lines.

Today, visitors come to Abilene to learn about its colorful past. Many people must find it hard to believe that once the streets there were crowded with cowboys. ■

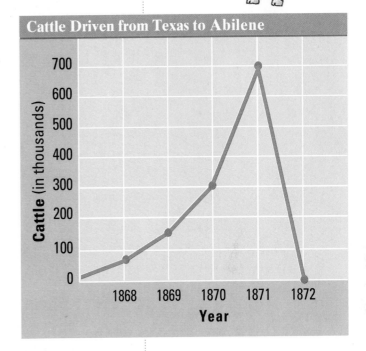

Cattle Driven from Texas to Abilene

■ *Why did Abilene's cattle business come to an end?*

REVIEW

1. **FOCUS** Why was Abilene known as a cattle town?
2. **CONNECT** Use the map on page 149 and the map on page 156 to find the Santa Fe Trail, the Oregon Trail, and the Chisholm Trail. Which trail crosses the most states?
3. **CRITICAL THINKING** What kinds of businesses do you think were harmed when cowboys stopped coming to Abilene?
4. **ACTIVITY** Draw a picture that shows some of the things you might have seen in Abilene in 1870. Then draw a picture that shows how the population and businesses had changed by 1872.

Using Grids

Here's Why You can use a map to locate any place on the earth. Suppose you want to find Wichita, Kansas. You may search on a map of Kansas until you find it. But there is a better, faster way. You can use a grid.

Here's How A grid is made of columns and rows that cross one another. Here is a grid on a map of Kansas. The columns on this grid have numbers. The rows have letters.

Use the grid to find Wichita. First, find row C. Then find column 5. Move your finger across row C until you come to column 5. Wichita is located in that area.

Can you locate Dodge City on the map of Kansas? It is in the C3 area. What city is located at B6 on the map? In which area of the map is Topeka located?

Kansas

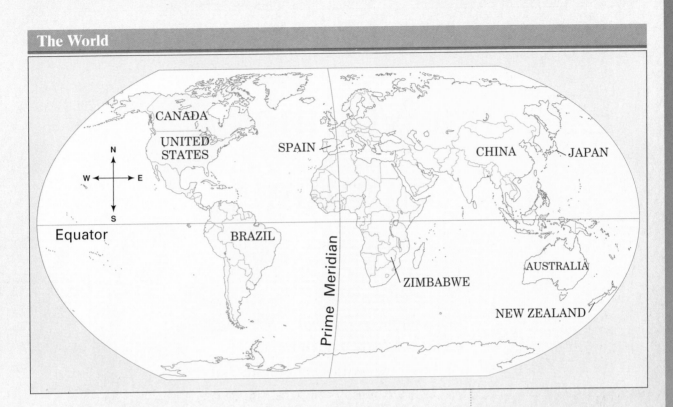

Many lines can be drawn on maps and globes to make grids. One of these lines goes around the globe halfway between the North Pole and the South Pole. It is called the equator. Another line goes from the North Pole to the South Pole. It is called the prime meridian. These are the two most important grid lines on maps and globes.

Look at the world map on this page. Find the United States. Is it north or south of the equator? Is the United States east or west of the prime meridian?

Try It Work with a partner. Use the world map on this page. Take turns naming places. Have the other person say whether your place is north or south of the equator and east or west of the prime meridian.

Apply It Use the world map on pages 232–233. Make a list of three countries that the equator runs through. List three countries that the prime meridian runs through.

Life in a Mining Community

THINKING FOCUS

Why was Leadville known as a boom town?

Key Terms

- vein
- mineral
- boom town

"We're rich! We're rich!" shouted the two miners in 1878. They jumped up and down with excitement.

Just a few days before, the two men had walked into a store in Leadville, Colorado. Their clothes were ragged, and they had everything they owned with them. They had come to Leadville hoping to find silver.

The two men asked the owner of the store for supplies. They had no money, so they agreed to give the store owner one-third of any silver they found.

Then the two men went off into the hills. Since it was a warm day, they began digging in a shady spot. A few days later, after digging down 27 feet, the men struck a large **vein,** or strip, of silver. If they had dug a little farther away in any direction, they would have missed the silver completely.

Now the two men—who had started out in rags—were as rich as kings. And there was a very happy store owner in Leadville!

Wealth of the Rockies

Leadville was not the only spot in the Rocky Mountains where gold and silver were found. The map below shows that valuable minerals were found in many places in the West. **Minerals** are materials such as gold and silver that are found in the earth. When news of the discoveries spread, people from all over the country came to the area.

Towns started wherever the mines were. The population of these mining towns grew even more rapidly when the railroad was built through the mountains. The railroad brought in miners, business people, and heavy machines needed in the mines. These mining towns were the first real settlements in the Rockies. ■

▼ *Leadville, Colorado, was one of many mining towns in the Rocky Mountains. This picture was taken in 1901.*

■ *Why did many towns spring up in the Rocky Mountains?*

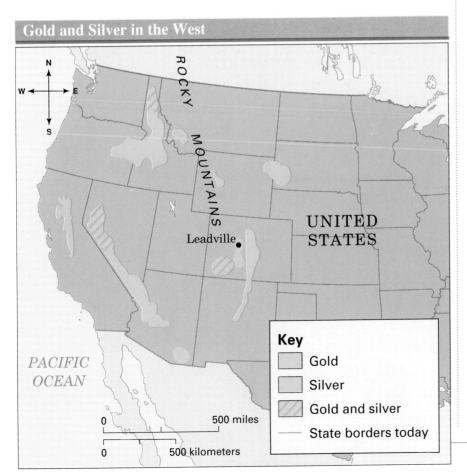

Gold and Silver in the West

ROCKY MOUNTAINS

UNITED STATES

Leadville

PACIFIC OCEAN

Key

Gold

Silver

Gold and silver

State borders today

0   500 miles

0   500 kilometers

A Boom Town

At the time that the two miners discovered silver, Leadville was a boom town. A **boom town** is a town that grows and becomes wealthy very quickly. News of the silver veins had spread quickly, and people poured into Leadville. Some people came hoping to find silver. Others came to earn money by working in mines owned by others. Business people came to open stores, hotels, and theaters for the new residents. In just one year, the population of Leadville rose from 300 people to 5,000 people!

Several silver veins were found near Leadville. Within one year, there were at least 12 silver mines in the area. People also mined gold, copper, and other valuable minerals. At one time, there were more than 240 mines around Leadville.

The rich residents of Leadville lived well, but not everyone made a lot of money. Many of the people who came to Leadville never found silver or any other valuable mineral. They often worked in mines for little money. ■

■ *What kind of people came to Leadville when it was known as a boom town?*

➤ *At this Leadville company, silver was melted and made into bars. Later, the silver could be made into coins, platters, cups, or other silver items.*

The Silver Runs Out

The boom in Leadville did not last. As the chart on this page shows, by 1916 Leadville had lost much of its population. One reason people left Leadville was that silver had become less valuable. Because mine owners were not making as much money selling silver as they had before, they could not pay their workers as much. The workers moved on to better paying jobs in other places.

People also left Leadville because most of the silver there had been removed from the earth and there were few new discoveries. People went to other places to look for minerals or to work in other mines. Many businesses closed because their customers were gone.

Leadville did not disappear, but its days as a boom town were over. It still attracts many visitors, though. They go to Leadville to enjoy the mountains and to learn about the interesting history of western mining towns. ∎

Population of Leadville	
Year	Population
1877	300
1878	5,000
1879	30,000
1900	12,500
1916	4,500
Present	4,000

▼ *The home of Horace Tabor still stands in Leadville today. Visitors can learn about this man who made a fortune from silver mines around Leadville during the 1800s.*

■ *What caused Leadville to go from a boom town to a quiet mountain town?*

R E V I E W

1. **FOCUS** Why was Leadville known as a boom town?
2. **CONNECT** Compare the way businesses changed in Abilene, Kansas, and in Leadville, Colorado.
3. **CRITICAL THINKING** Pretend you have just arrived in Leadville and you want to be a miner. What questions would you ask the people in the town about Leadville and about mining?
4. **ACTIVITY** Pretend you are living in the East in 1879. You have heard about Leadville and its silver mines, and you have been given a free railroad ticket to go there. Will you use the ticket? Discuss your answer with your classmates.

Chapter Review

Reviewing Key Terms

blaze (p. 136)
boom town (p. 162)
mineral (p. 161)
pass (p. 148)
pioneer (p. 135)

population (p. 155)
trade center (p. 156)
wagon train (p. 149)
vein (p. 160)

A. Choose the word that best completes the sentence.

1. Pioneers went through a (pass, vein) to get across a steep mountain.
2. A (mineral, population) is usually found in the earth.
3. A (pioneer, vein) is a long strip of a mineral.
4. (Sailors, Pioneers) left settled places and moved to the wilderness.
5. After most of the silver was mined, the (population, pass) of Leadville got smaller.
6. Pioneers traveled along the Oregon Trail in (boats, wagon trains).
7. People buy and sell goods at a (wagon train, trade center).
8. Daniel Boone (closed, blazed) a trail from Virginia to Kentucky.
9. A (mineral, boom town) grows quickly.

Exploring Concepts

1. Pioneers moved to Kentucky and other places for different reasons. Copy and complete the chart to show why they moved.
2. Explain why Daniel Boone's work on the Wilderness Trail was important to the pioneers who moved west.
3. List three problems that pioneers on the Oregon Trail had.
4. How did the railroad help the town of Abilene grow?

Where pioneers moved	Why they moved there
Kentucky	
Leadville	
Oregon	
Santa Fe	

Reviewing Skills

1. Look at the map of New Mexico on the right. Using the grid, tell what area Santa Fe is in. Locate Gallup. Where is Hobbs?

2. Use the political map on pages 232–233 to name two countries south of the equator.

3. Look at the map on page 156. What direction do you travel if you go from Abilene to San Antonio?

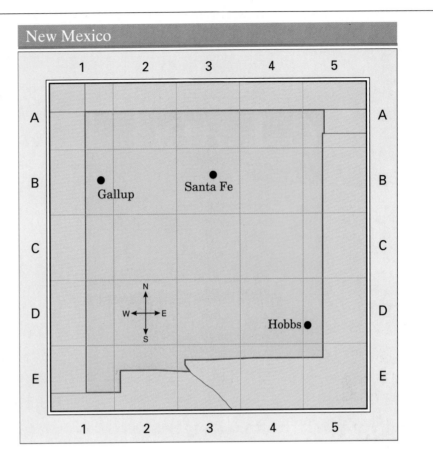

New Mexico

Using Critical Thinking

1. Sometimes a wagon broke down on the rough trails and could not be fixed. What do you think pioneers did when their wagons broke down?

2. When most of the minerals were dug up in Leadville, miners had no jobs and many people had to move away. Where do you think those people moved to? What do you think they did to earn a living?

Preparing for Citizenship

1. **ART ACTIVITY** Pretend you traveled on the Chisholm Trail. Draw a picture of something you saw on the trail. Put your picture with those of your classmates to make a long mural.

2. **COLLABORATIVE LEARNING** As a class project, do a live news report about crossing the mountains in a wagon train. Three students should be the TV reporters. The rest of the students should tell the reporters what happened to them on their trip across the mountains.

The Land Today

The United States is a land of plenty with vast resources stretching from sea to sea. Today, its people and cities use many of the same resources that fed, clothed, and sheltered the American Indians and pioneers of long ago. New ways of farming, making products, and moving goods to market help provide what today's growing population needs to live. These resources, however, cannot last forever. If we want to protect the beauty and the resources of our country, we must care for our land and all that it stands for.

166

Kinuko Y. Craft. Watercolor and oil. Shown at Stars and Stripes exhibit at the American Institute of Graphic Arts, San Francisco.

Chapter 9

The Land of Plenty

Can you imagine having to grow your own food and build your own home? The Indians and pioneers had to do this to survive. Today we can depend on other people to farm the land and make building materials. Modern farms and businesses produce goods that are shipped across the country to people who need them. Our land of plenty provides all that we need to live.

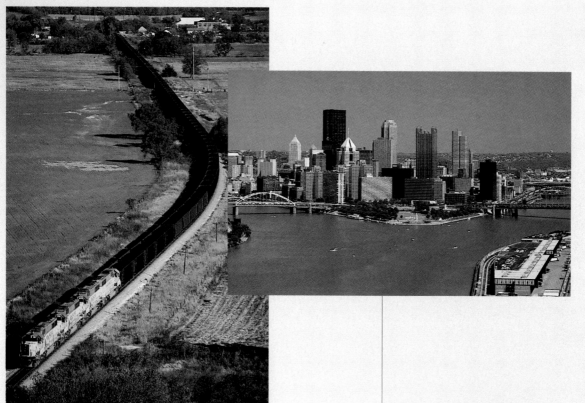

Train engines can pull many rail cars at the same time. Trains carry all kinds of goods from livestock to food to automobiles.

Pittsburgh, Pennsylvania, is built near three rivers and large amounts of coal. This location helped it become a major producer of the world's steel.

The San Joaquin
(SAN waw KEEN) Valley
produces half of the fruits
and vegetables eaten in the
United States. This valley
also produces crops such as
the cotton shown above.

All farmers in the San Joaquin
Valley depend on water
brought in from other areas to
water their crops.

Farming in the San Joaquin Valley

Key Terms

- agriculture
- irrigation
- fertilizer

➤ *This machine shakes almond trees so that the nuts fall to the ground. Later, the outer layer of the almonds will be peeled away. When the nuts are sent to stores, they look like the ones above.*

P edro Cruz struggled to hold the heavy bag of almonds.

"Here, let me help you," offered his older sister Rosa.

"No, no," said Pedro. "I'm fine."

Rosa smiled, knowing that Pedro was excited. Both children were on their way to Mexico to see their uncle. Pedro wanted to give him the almonds himself.

The Cruzes had left Mexico to become citizens of the United States. At first Pedro and Rosa's parents moved from state to state picking crops. Now the family lived and worked all year on a farm near Bakersfield, California.

"There it is!" shouted Pedro, pointing to the bus that would take them from Bakersfield to Mexico. He lifted his bag of almonds high, trying to control his excitement!

Rich Soil

Workers like the Cruzes harvest many different crops grown near Bakersfield. One half of the fresh fruits, nuts, and vegetables that are grown in the United States comes from the area known as the San Joaquin Valley. This land is north of Bakersfield in the central part of California.

Find the San Joaquin Valley on the map. Notice that the San Joaquin River runs through this land. Between which two rows of mountains does the San Joaquin Valley lie?

What makes the San Joaquin Valley so good for growing crops? The soil is good for plants. For thousands of years, streams and rivers from nearby mountains have carried rich soil down to the valley. Also, whenever rivers in the area overflowed, they added new soil to the land. Plants grow very well in this rich soil.

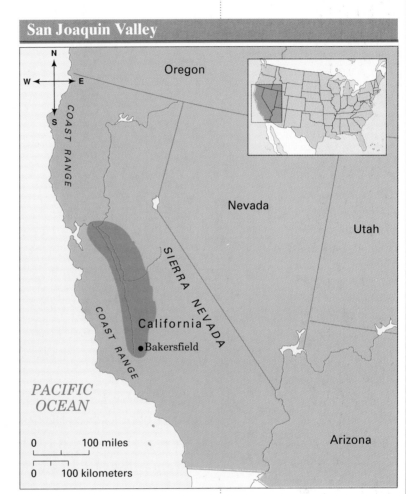

San Joaquin Valley

More than just rich soil makes the San Joaquin Valley good for **agriculture,** which is the business of farming. The valley also has a good climate in which to grow crops. The spring and fall are warm, and the summer is hot but dry. Winter is cool and wet. Temperatures rarely drop below freezing. With enough water, crops can grow all year in this climate.

Look at the lists on page 172. They show the four kinds of agricultural products that come from the San Joaquin Valley. What are these products? ■

■ *What makes the San Joaquin Valley a good place for farming?*

171

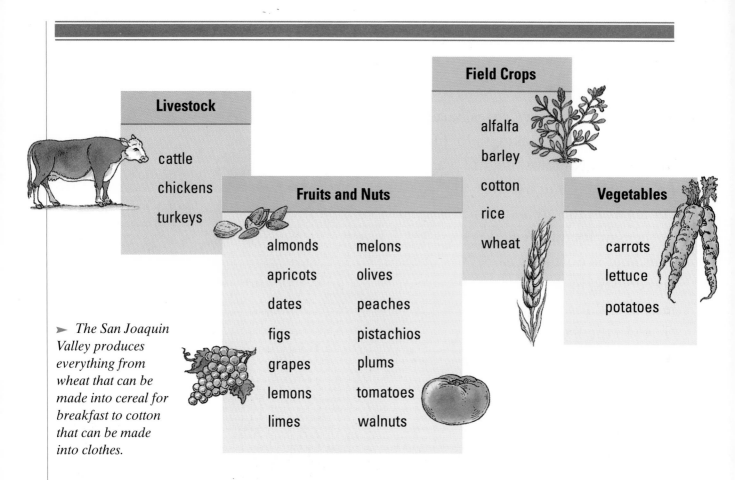

Livestock

cattle

chickens

turkeys

Fruits and Nuts

almonds	melons
apricots	olives
dates	peaches
figs	pistachios
grapes	plums
lemons	tomatoes
limes	walnuts

Field Crops

alfalfa

barley

cotton

rice

wheat

Vegetables

carrots

lettuce

potatoes

➤ *The San Joaquin Valley produces everything from wheat that can be made into cereal for breakfast to cotton that can be made into clothes.*

Working the Land

Are rich soil and a good climate enough to produce such big crops? No. Plants also need lots of water. However, almost half of the San Joaquin Valley is desert. You remember that few plants grow well in deserts because there is not much rain. In the summer, the most important growing season, the San Joaquin Valley gets almost no rain.

How can the farmers in the San Joaquin Valley grow crops in such a dry place? They bring in water from other parts of California. Much of this water comes from the mountains in parts of northern and eastern California. The water is carried from the mountains to the valley through pipes, ditches, or canals. Bringing water to dry land is called **irrigation.**

Rich soil, a good climate, and irrigation help grow strong plants. Farmers also help plants grow by adding fertilizers to the soil. **Fertilizers** are chemicals that feed plants and make them grow stronger and more quickly.

Across Time & Space

Irrigation is not new. Over 1,000 years ago, Indians used ditches to bring water to huge areas of land in central Arizona.

172

Many farmers spray crops with chemicals that attack weeds and insects. These chemicals help farmers keep crops healthy and free from weeds. Some chemicals that farmers use are dangerous to people and animals, so many farmers try to use those that are safest. ■

■ *How do chemicals and irrigation help farmers?*

▼ *California produces more lemons than any other state in the United States.*

Harvesting the Crops

Once crops are grown, they are harvested. Some crops are harvested by machines, which make the job quick and easy. However, large machines can damage certain crops. Therefore, some crops, like grapes, melons, and lemons, must be carefully harvested by people.

When the crops are ready, families like the Cruzes gather in an area and begin the hard job of harvesting. Thousands of farm workers are hired to pick the crops. The work is long and hard. Often, the living conditions near fields are poor.

After the crops are picked, they are packed and placed on trucks and trains. Products from the San Joaquin Valley are then sent to people throughout the country. ■

■ *How are farmers able to harvest so many crops?*

R E V I E W

1. **FOCUS** What kinds of crops grow in the San Joaquin Valley, and why do they grow so well?
2. **CONNECT** Compare how people use the land of the San Joaquin Valley with the way the Kwakiutl used the land.
3. **CRITICAL THINKING** Why do you think people in many states might worry if insects destroyed crops in the San Joaquin Valley?
4. **ACTIVITY** Look at the lists on page 172. Make your own list of products you have eaten recently that might have come from the San Joaquin Valley.

Getting Farm Products to Stores

You know that many different crops are grown in the San Joaquin Valley of California. You know why they grow so well there. You also know how they are harvested. But do you know how they get from a farm to stores across the country? Let's think about that a little bit.

Here's Why

Suppose you grow almonds, tomatoes, and carrots on a farm in the San Joaquin Valley. You want to send them to cities in the United States and then to stores within the cities. You have to decide how to get your crops to the stores at the lowest cost before they spoil or rot. How will you send each of them?

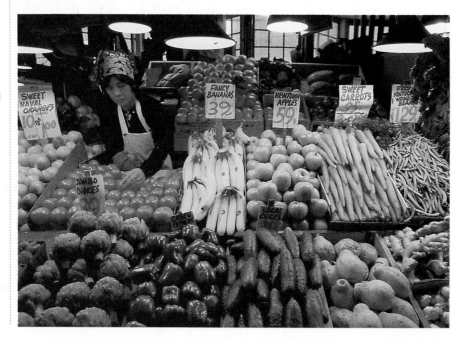

Here's How

Your crops can be shipped by truck, airplane, or train. You may have to use more than one method of transportation. Use the chart below to help you decide how to ship your crops.

Comparing Ways of Moving Farm Products

Airplane
Travels faster than trucks or trains.
Costs more than trucks or trains.
Cannot carry products directly to stores.

Truck
Costs less than airplanes or trains.
Can carry products directly to stores.
Travels slower than airplanes and trains.

Train
Can carry more than airplanes or trucks.
Costs more than trucks.
Cannot carry products directly to stores.

Try It

Work with a partner. Discuss how to get your three crops to stores where you now live. Write four or more questions that you must answer before you can decide. One question might be: How much will it cost?

Apply It

Now, make your decision. Write a report that tells how you will get each of your three crops to stores. Tell why you made your decision.

Using Tables

Here's Why   You know that half of our country's fruits and vegetables come from the San Joaquin Valley in California. But what about grain crops, such as the wheat in the picture below? How much grain does California produce? How does its grain production compare with other states? One way you could find this information is to look at a table.

Here's How   A table is one way to organize number information so that it can be understood easily. Look at the table on the next page. It gives grain production from five states for the year 1986. What are the five states? Four grain crops are listed in the table. What are the four crops? Notice that each number shows how many millions of bushels are produced. One million is a large number: 1,000,000.

How can you find out how much of each crop a state produced in 1986? Find the name of the state on the left. Find the name of the crop at the top. Move your finger across the page until you come to the column for the crop you want. For example, to find how much corn was grown in California, go across the California row until you come to the corn column. The number in that space is the number of millions of bushels of corn grown in California in 1986. What is that number?

176

Grain Production in Millions of Bushels — 1986

States	Barley	Corn	Oats	Wheat
California	24	38	3	52
Colorado	21	99	3	96
Kansas	10	182	11	433
Ohio	1	476	12	48
Texas	2	149	8	120

Try It Use the table to compare states. For example, if you look at the column of numbers under *wheat,* you can see that Kansas grew the most wheat of these five states. How many millions of bushels of wheat did Kansas grow? Which of these five states grew the smallest amount of wheat? How many millions of bushels of wheat did that state grow?

Apply It Write three questions that can be answered from the table. Then work with a partner. Ask your partner to find the information in the table that answers your questions. Find the information that answers your partner's three questions.

Steel in Pittsburgh

Why is Pittsburgh in a good location for making steel?

Key Terms

- location
- steel mills
- industry
- services

➤ *In 1930, Thomas Hart Benton painted* Steel. *It shows the inside of a steel mill. What do you think working in a mill would sound like?*

People like to invent tall tales about their heros. In Pittsburgh, Pennsylvania, a city famous for making steel, people tell stories about Joe Magarac. They say he was the greatest steel worker of all.

Joe Magarac was seven feet of solid steel from head to toe. He worked in a factory, mixing and pouring gallons of bubbling hot steel into big tubs. He stopped only to eat five or six meals a day. Joe stirred the red-hot steel with his bare hands. He would scoop it up and make eight long railroad rails at the same time. He'd squeeze them out from between his fingers, four from each hand.

Joe Magarac wasn't real, of course, but the tale of Joe Magarac shows that steelworkers are American heros.

Steel City

Steel is a very strong metal. It is so strong that people use it to make cars, airplanes, trains, bridges, buildings, and all kinds of machines we use every day. The city that became best known for making steel is Pittsburgh. It is still called "Steel City."

One reason Pittsburgh became Steel City is that it is in a good location for making steel. The place where something is found is its **location.** Pittsburgh's location is good because it is close to natural resources that people use to make steel.

The most important natural resources near Pittsburgh are its rivers and its coal and iron. Find Pittsburgh's three rivers on the map. Miners dig the coal and iron from the earth nearby. These are then shipped on the rivers to Pittsburgh. Here, people who work in **steel mills,** which are factories that make steel, use the coal and iron to make steel. The steel is then shipped out to the world by ships or by trains. ◼

▼ By 1904 there were over 30 steel mills. In the 1970s more steel was produced than ever before. But in the 1980s the number of mills dropped down to three.

Pittsburgh Area Steel Mills

0   50 miles

0   50 kilometers

Pennsylvania

Ohio River

Allegheny River

Pittsburgh

Monongahela River

N
W   E
S

Key

▢ Pittsburgh

🏭 Mills in early 1900s

◼ How did Pittsburgh's location by three rivers help its steel industry?

Pittsburgh Grows

The steel **industry,** or business, helped make Pittsburgh great. Many people moved to Pittsburgh during the early 1900s to get jobs working in the steel industry. Because the steelworkers needed food, clothing, houses, and other goods, more people came to Pittsburgh to provide these things. For years, the city grew and grew.

This view of Pittsburgh in 1911 shows smoky air from the steel mills.

This photograph shows a clear view of Pittsburgh today. What made the difference?

■ *What problems did the steel industry cause?*

Over time, the amount of steel produced in Pittsburgh grew. With so many mills, there also came problems.

One problem was dirty air. To make steel, coal is burned. Burning coal sends off smoke. Pittsburgh used to have air filled with smoke. People didn't like living in smoky air. So in 1946, Pittsburgh began a smoke-control program. By 1960, the city had clean air again.

However, Pittsburgh faced another problem in the 1980s. Factories in other parts of the world also made steel. Other countries could make steel cheaper, so most of the steel mills in Steel City closed down. ■

New Beginnings

The people of Pittsburgh went to work to solve this problem, too. They rebuilt the machines in their mills and found new ways to make steel more cheaply. People also started new industries in Pittsburgh, such as computer

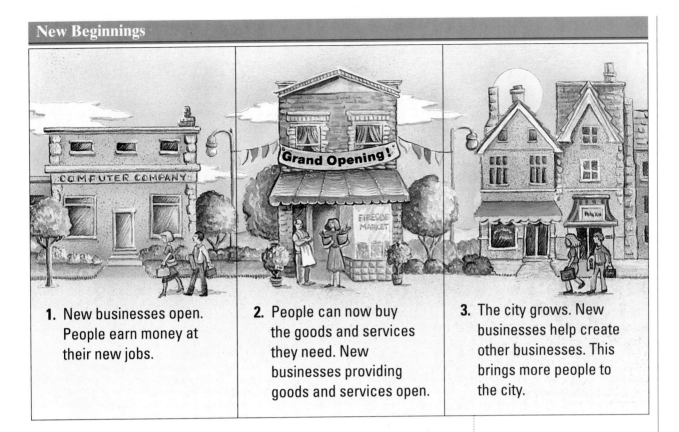

1. New businesses open. People earn money at their new jobs.

2. People can now buy the goods and services they need. New businesses providing goods and services open.

3. The city grows. New businesses help create other businesses. This brings more people to the city.

companies. Soon, more people got jobs in these new businesses.

The chart above shows how new businesses help a city grow. When new businesses open, people move nearby to work. With more people living in an area, more new businesses are needed to serve these people. **Services—** stores, schools, restaurants, gas stations—are businesses that provide people with what they need to live.

In this way, Pittsburgh has been able to keep growing. Some people think that Pittsburgh is one of the best cities in the United States in which to live. Joe Magarac would be proud of this city and how it has grown. ■

■ *In what ways has Pittsburgh kept growing?*

R E V I E W

1. **FOCUS** Why is Pittsburgh in a good location for making steel?
2. **CONNECT** How does the workplace of a steelworker in Pittsburgh differ from the workplace of a farm worker in the San Joaquin Valley?
3. **CRITICAL THINKING** Why is it important for people in a city to try to make the air

clean and safe?
4. **WRITING ACTIVITY** Make a list of people you have seen working in services, such as bank tellers and secretaries. Next to it, write the businesses that they would work in, such as banks and offices.

Moving by Rail

THINKING
FOCUS

How do trains help move goods and people across America?

Key Terms

- freight
- trade
- transportation

Travel

The railroad track is
   miles away,
And the day is loud
   with voices speaking,
Yet there isn't a train
   goes by all day
But I hear its whistle
   shrieking.

All night there isn't a
   train goes by,
Though the night is still
   for sleep and dreaming,
But I see its cinders red
   on the sky,
And hear its engine
   steaming.

My heart is warm with
   the friends I make,
And better friends I'll not
   be knowing;
Yet there isn't a train I
   wouldn't take,
No matter where it's going.

        Edna St. Vincent Millay

This poem captures a good feeling that Americans have about trains. Trains remind us of faraway places that we'd like to visit. However, trains are useful to us in ways that are practical, too.

Trains and Other Ways to Travel

In this chapter you read about farming in the San Joaquin Valley and making steel in Pittsburgh. How do products like farm goods and steel get from where they are grown or made to where people use them?

Many things people need are shipped by train. Trains that carry **freight**—that is, goods like steel and almonds—are called freight trains. Trains that carry people when they travel are called passenger trains. A passenger is a person who rides from place to place.

◀ *This engine got its power from steam. It burned wood or coal to boil water. The steam from the boiling water ran the engine.*

▼ *This advertisement for the St. Louis and San Francisco railroad line shows a brother and sister waiting in the station, ready for a journey by train.*

People have been using freight and passenger trains since the late 1860s, when railroads first crossed the nation from coast to coast. Trains became popular because they made traveling much faster. For example, in the 1880s a trip from Chicago to Denver in a horse-drawn buggy could take 49 days. The same trip by train took only six days, and it was a lot less bumpy!

By the 1920s, however, a new invention became popular, the automobile. Many Americans bought cars so they could travel wherever they wanted. They did not have to take trains, which went only to certain places.

In the 1950s, many people started to travel by airplane because it was even faster. At that time, a person could fly in a plane from New York to Los Angeles in 18 hours. The same trip by train would take three to four days. ■

Railroads Today

Trains aren't as fast as planes and can't go everywhere that cars and trucks do, but they are still used because they cost less and can carry more. Trains move many of the goods people buy and sell. Buying and selling goods is called **trade.** Trains, ships, trucks, and airplanes help trade. These forms of **transportation,** or ways of moving things, take goods from place to place. Trains help trade between distant states in the United States.

Today, people use what is called "piggybacking" to load freight. Workers can load a box full of goods onto a train car, then stack another box, piggyback, on top of that one. This way, trains are even more useful since twice as many loads can be carried at the same time.

Ships, trains, and trucks work together to move freight. At a seaport, you might see boxes of tuna fish being unloaded from a ship. Those boxes might be put on a freight train and taken to a distant city. Then, they might be loaded on a truck to be delivered to a store near you.

On the next page, you can read more about freight trains—how they move and what they carry.

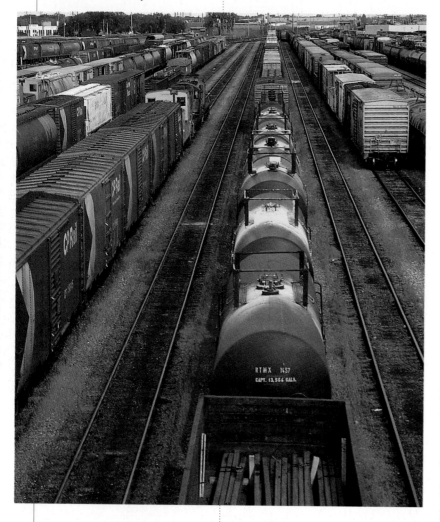

▼ This is a freight yard. These cars are waiting to be loaded and hooked up to engines so their goods can be delivered across the country.

A Freight Train

Modern freight trains have many cars that are used for different purposes. These cars are used to move everything from tanks of liquids to livestock to coal.

Stacked three high, this car carries up to 18 automobiles. Today, freight trains move six out of every ten new automobiles made in the United States.

Piggyback boxcars carry peaches from factories where they were canned to cities where they will be sold. A boxcar is a closed train car that carries almost anything.

An engine leads the way! It has the power to pull all the cars. This modern engine runs on diesel *(DEE zuhl)*, a form of oil. The engineer controls how fast the train goes.

185

➤ *This chart compares travel by steam train and horse before 1929 and between modern trains and airplanes. How many miles per hour can a modern train go compared to a steam-powered train?*

Travel Now and in the Past

550 miles per hour

79 miles per hour

21 miles per hour

3 miles per hour

✈	Jet airplane
🚂	Modern train
🚂	Steam train
🐎	Horse and buggy

▲ *The TGV is a bullet train that travels from Paris to Lyon, France. Its name means "great speed" in French because it can travel 168 miles per hour. How much faster is that than U.S. trains?*

■ *How are railroads helping businesses today?*

Today, most Americans travel long distances by car, bus, or airplane. Compare how much faster airplanes are than trains on the chart above. Even so, people still do ride trains. In 1970, a new passenger railroad called Amtrak began. The name "Amtrak" comes from "**Am**erica," "**tra**vel," and "trac**k**." Thousands ride Amtrak for short trips, often to get to and from work.

People are inventing new kinds of trains, too. One type of new train, called a bullet train, can travel very fast. In the future, bullet trains may carry people to jobs far away from their homes. Because the trains are so fast, people will be able to get to and from work more quickly than ever. ■

R E V I E W

1. **FOCUS** How do trains help move goods and people across the United States?
2. **CONNECT** How might very fast freight trains be helpful to farmers in the San Joaquin Valley?
3. **CRITICAL THINKING** What do you think would happen to the transportation industry if someone invented a faster and cheaper way of moving goods?
4. **ACTIVITY** Work with a group. Make a model freight train out of shoeboxes. Draw on a shoebox to make it look like a certain type of train car. Load your train car with freight. Decide where it is going and then tell the class.

Trade Among Countries

Some food grown in California is sold to other states. Some of it is sold to other countries. The United States buys products from other countries, too. The buying and selling of products among countries is called international trade.

Products that a country sells to another country are called exports. Products that a country buys from another country are called imports. Exports go out. Imports come in.

The United States trades with many countries around the world. Canada is the largest trade partner of the United States. In fact, Canada and the United States sell more products to each other than do any other two countries in the world. Some of these products are shown on the map below.

International trade is important to most countries. When countries export products, they earn money. When they import products, they get things they need.

Trade Between the United States and Canada

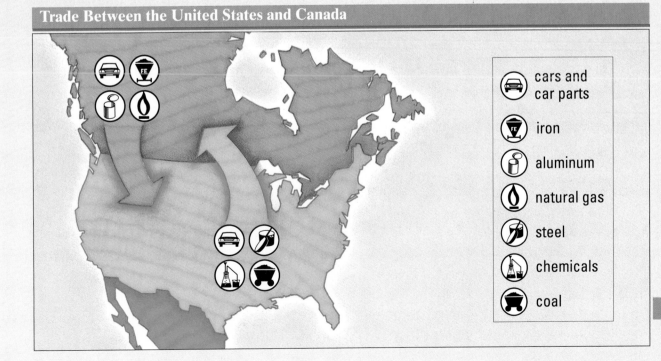

cars and car parts
iron
aluminum
natural gas
steel
chemicals
coal

Chapter Review

Reviewing Key Terms

agriculture (p. 171)   location (p. 179)
fertilizer (p. 172)   services (p. 181)
freight (p. 183)   steel mills (p. 179)
industry (p. 179)   trade (p. 184)
irrigation (p. 172)   transportation (p. 184)

A. Write the key term for each meaning.

1. where something is found
2. businesses that perform work or provide people with what they need to live
3. the business of farming
4. materials that are carried by train, ship, truck, or plane
5. factories that make steel
6. chemicals that make plants grow strong and more quickly
7. the buying and selling of goods
8. a business that makes things to sell
9. a way of moving goods or passengers
10. the bringing of water to dry land

Exploring Concepts

A. Copy the timeline below. On your timeline, show when trains, automobiles, and airplanes began to be used a lot for travel. Draw a picture for each of the three dates.

B. Answer each question at the right with one or two sentences.

1. How can crops grow in dry areas like the San Joaquin Valley?
2. Usually a city grows and is a good place to live if there are plenty of jobs for people. Why do you think this is true?
3. Explain how trains and trucks work together to move freight.

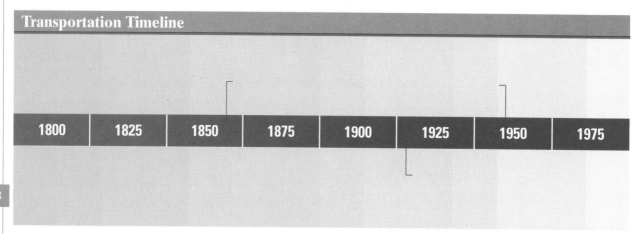

Transportation Timeline

| 1800 | 1825 | 1850 | 1875 | 1900 | 1925 | 1950 | 1975 |

Reviewing Skills

1. The table below shows the amount of land used to grow the main agricultural crops in three states. Write three sentences about what the table shows.

2. Look at the physical map on pages 238–239. What physical features are in Alabama?

State	Thousands of Acres
California	4,922
Alabama	2,267
Arizona	738

Using Critical Thinking

1. Many crops are grown in California and shipped to other states. Why do you think strawberries are not shipped the same way as cotton? How do you think strawberries and cotton are each shipped?

2. In big cities, the air is made dirty by automobile engines. What would you suggest to help solve this problem?

Preparing for Citizenship

1. **COLLECTING INFORMATION** Work with a partner. Prepare a scrapbook of pictures of goods made of steel. Look through old magazines to find as many pictures as you can.

2. **COLLABORATIVE LEARNING** Many tall-tale characters are heroes to certain industries. For example, Joe Magarac is a hero to steelmakers, John Henry is a hero to railroaders, and Paul Bunyan is a hero to lumberjacks. Make up your own classroom tall-tale hero. Brainstorm the kinds of things your hero would do. Work in small groups to write stories. Put all the stories together to make a classroom book. Vote on a title for your book. Choose someone to draw a cover.

Chapter 10

Taking Care of Our Land

Our country is a land of great natural beauty. But today we are using resources rapidly and producing large amounts of trash and poisons that harm our land. To protect the beauty of our land, many people are working to clean up our environment and to find ways to use resources wisely.

These stacks of old boxes will be made into new cardboard items and used again. That means fewer trees will be cut down to make new cardboard.

Every year, more and more people in the United States are saving old newspapers and other kinds of trash that can be used again or made into something new.

If we all work together to clean up our resources, more areas can become as clean and beautiful as this protected land in one of our many national parks.

Every day we use clean water in our homes. If we try to use less water each time, we are helping to save our clean water resources.

A tree stump is a home to insects, a scratching post for bears, and a place where people can rest. So who really owns the tree stump? Read a story that answers this question about the land.

LITERATURE

ONCE THERE WAS A TREE

Written by Natalia Romanova

Adapted by Anne Schwartz

Illustrated by Gennady Spirin

Once there was a tree. It had grown for many years and now it was growing old.

Dark clouds swept across the sky. Rain fell, thunder roared, and a lightning bolt split the tree in two.

A woodsman came upon the broken tree and sawed it down so that only the stump remained. Soon a bark beetle with long feelers settled in. The beetle loved the stump and laid her eggs under its bark.

The eggs hatched and tiny maggots emerged. All summer long they gnawed tunnels in the bark. Winter came and they slept. When they awoke in the spring with long feelers of their own, it was time to fly away.

But the tree stump was not deserted for long. With
all the entrances and exits the maggots had made, here
was the perfect place for ants to live. One ant brought a
leaf, another a twig, and another a grain of
sand. They cleared out the tunnels
and made the stump their home.
A bear approached the
tree stump, sniffed at it, and
sharpened her claws on the
bark. The stump was hers,
like everything else around.
Even the ants in the stump
were hers, and no other bear
would dare disturb them.

A titmouse flew down and landed on the stump. She spotted an ant dragging a caterpillar and pecked at it. Now the caterpillar was hers. The ants were hers, too, and so was the tree stump. No other birds would come near.

One rainy day a frog found shelter in a hole in the tree stump. Time and weather had dug these holes, which would protect others who also passed by.

The warm sun dried the tree stump, and soon a new occupant had moved in— an earwig. Liking nothing better than the shade, he crept under the bark to sleep.

A man was walking in the woods and saw the tree stump. He sat down on it to rest, and now the tree stump was his.

The man thought he owned the forest—and the earth—so why not the tree stump?

But who really owns the tree stump? The bark beetle that gnaws tunnels inside it? The ants that travel through the tunnels? The earwig that sleeps under its bark? Or the bear that uses it to sharpen her claws?

Does it belong to the titmouse that flies down upon it? The frog that finds shelter in one of its holes? Or the man who believes he owns the forest?

Maybe the tree stump belongs to all—the beetle and the ants, the bear and the titmouse, the frog, the earwig, and even the man. All must live together.

Meanwhile the tree stump gets older and older. The sun warms it; the rain cools it. Soon it begins to rot. Night comes, and the forest is cast in moonlight. What remains of the tree stump glows in the dark.

Now the tree stump is gone. A new tree has grown in its place. A titmouse is perched in its branches—it is her tree. An ant crawls up high—on her tree. A bear lumbers by and sharpens his claws on the bark. A man lies down to rest in its shade. The tree belongs to all, because it grows from the earth that is home for all.

Saving Our Land

How can we conserve our natural resources?

Key Terms

- topsoil
- conservation
- environment

➤ *This picture shows a dust storm that took place in Hugoton, Kansas, in 1937.*

M other, what is that?" asks Ellie, pointing to a dark cloud moving toward the house.

"It's a dust storm!" shouts Mother. "Quick! Shut the door!"

Ellie bolts the door and helps her mother close the windows. Just as the last one is latched, the storm hits.

The afternoon becomes dark as dust blocks the sun. Outside, it is almost impossible to see or breathe. Even inside the small farmhouse, dust begins to form layers.

The next morning, all is quiet. Ellie opens the door a crack and looks outside. Dust still falls slowly from the sky. A layer of dust covers the barn, the fence, and even the clothesline. It lies like a thick blanket over the land.

The Need to Protect Land

In the 1930s, strong winds swept across much of the Great Plains. The winds picked up soil from the dry earth, creating huge clouds of dust. The map shows where these storms were. This area was known as the Dust Bowl.

Dust storms wear away the top layer of soil, called **topsoil.** These storms usually happen when land is very dry and when there are not enough plants to hold topsoil in place. Dusty, loose soil can be swept away by strong winds.

Land and water are important natural resources. Events like the storms that took place in the Dust Bowl called attention to the need to conserve these resources.

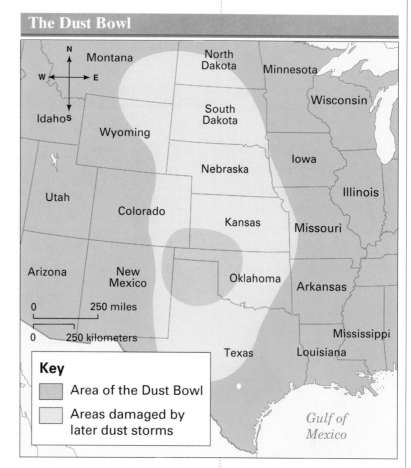

The Dust Bowl

Key
Area of the Dust Bowl
Areas damaged by later dust storms

The darker orange area on the map shows the Dust Bowl. Why do you think it was called a bowl?

Conservation Efforts

When the early settlers spread out across the United States, they were amazed by the richness of the land. They saw forests that spread out for miles and miles. The prairies they traveled seemed to be endless.

Today, however, we know that our resources are not endless and that we need to protect them. Protecting our natural resources is called **conservation.**

There are many different ways of protecting our resources. Over a hundred years ago, the leaders of our country began to conserve some wilderness areas. Some of these are called national parks. The land there is protected from changes. On the next pages, you will read about some of these national parks. ■

■ Why do we need to protect our land?

National Parks

In 1872, the United States government began to set aside certain wilderness areas that would not be changed by people. Since plant and animal life in these areas is protected, visitors can enjoy the land's natural beauty.

Planning a vacation? This map shows national parks across the United States. Use it to find the three national parks pictured on these two pages. Which of these three parks is nearest you?

U.S. National Parks

Denali National Park

N
W E
S

Yellowstone National Park

PACIFIC OCEAN

Hawaii Volcanoes National Park

ATLANTIC OCEAN

Gulf of Mexico

The first national park in the United States was Yellowstone National Park in Wyoming, Idaho, and Montana. It has thousands of hot springs. Some springs are so hot the water boils. Others shoot water and steam from deep in the ground a hundred feet into the air. These fountains of hot water are called geysers *(GY zuhrz)*.

The highest peak in North America, Mount McKinley, stands in Denali National Park in Alaska. There are also many other mountains in the park. Moose, deer, and other wildlife roam the land there.

Red-hot lava spouts from Kilauea *(kee low AY uh).* It is a volcano in Hawaii Volcanoes National Park.

This rock was formed when hot lava, which is melted rock from inside the earth, poured from a volcano, cooled, and hardened.

Conserving Our Resources

We must conserve all of our natural resources. For example, we need rich topsoil to grow food for people and livestock. Plants grow very well in areas with rich topsoil. That is why farmers are so concerned with soil conservation. Look at the chart below to learn ways that farmers conserve topsoil on farmland.

Four Ways That Farmers Conserve Soil

Farmers plant rows of trees, called windbreaks, along the edge of fields. The trees slow the wind so it doesn't cause dust storms.

Farmers plow across hills so that plowed soil forms ridges. The ridges catch the water so it doesn't run downhill and erode the soil.

Farmers cut off a crop and leave the lower part of the plants behind. The roots of these plants hold the soil in place so that rain cannot wash it away.

Farmers plant crops in strips. A crop that holds water well is placed next to a crop that does not. The plants that hold water keep the water from washing soil away.

The conservation of our forests is also important. Forests give us wood for lumber, paper, and much more. They also provide homes for many animals. We can help conserve forests by limiting how many trees are cut. We can also plant new trees where they have been cut down.

You can help conserve forests by using paper wisely. Use paper plates and cups only when you have to. Write on both sides of a piece of notebook paper before throwing it away.

Water is another important resource. People, plants, and animals need water to live. What can you do to conserve water? Try not to waste it. Take shorter showers and turn off the water while you brush your teeth.

Conserving soil, trees, and water helps to create a healthy environment. All the things that surround us — air, water, and land— are a part of our **environment.** We must do more than conserve our natural resources. We must also try to clean those resources that have become too dirty to use. In the next lesson, you will read about what you can do to keep our environment clean. ■

■ *List three natural resources and tell what people can do to conserve them.*

◄ *National forests are areas that are taken care of by the United States government. Trees in national forests can be cut down, but the government makes sure that new trees are planted to replace them.*

R E V I E W

1. **FOCUS** How can we conserve our natural resources?
2. **CONNECT** How does farming in the San Joaquin Valley depend on natural resources?
3. **CRITICAL THINKING** How would your life be different if the place where you live had very little water?
4. **ACTIVITY** Work with a partner. List some of the kinds of plants that need topsoil. Then make a list of the things that can be made from these plants. Finally, tell why topsoil is important.

Protecting Our Resources

THINKING
FOCUS

Why is it important to lower the amount of pollution?

Key Terms

- pollution
- waste

➤ *This animal rescue worker is holding a sea otter that was once covered with oil.*

In the spring of 1989, rescue teams rushed to Alaska. A ship had accidentally spilled millions of gallons of oil into the ocean, harming the plant and animal life there.

Many rescue workers were worried about sea otters. Otters have thick fur that keeps them warm in cold water. When their fur gets oily, however, otters can no longer stay warm. Otters also lick their fur clean. The oil that otters were swallowing was poisoning them.

First, the workers had to catch the otters. Then they washed off the oil with dish detergent. The teams worked hard to save the otters. Many otters died, but thanks to the workers, many healthy otters returned to the sea.

Pollution

In the last lesson, you read about conserving our natural resources. An important part of conservation is keeping our environment clean. Oil spills like the one in Alaska cause pollution. When harmful chemicals make the air, water, or soil unhealthy or poisonous, it is called **pollution.** Besides accidental oil spills, there are other types of pollution that happen every day.

Cars and factories create air pollution. When car engines burn gasoline, they give off poisons that make the air dirty. Some of the smoke that comes from factories also pollutes the air. This type of pollution is harmful to plants and animals, including people.

Air pollution makes the air hard to breathe. It can hurt our lungs and sting our eyes. Sometimes pollution can weaken or kill trees and other plants. It can even wear away the stone in buildings. If this pollution gets into the water of lakes and streams, it can harm animal and plant life there.

◀ *Often, the pollution in air cannot be seen, but it can be harmful enough to eat away stone, as on the arm of this statue. You can also see from this leaf how pollution that gets into rain water can harm trees.*

Other kinds of water pollution can be caused by communities or factories dumping waste into oceans, rivers, and lakes. **Waste** includes things we don't need anymore and want to throw away, such as garbage and harmful chemicals. Water pollution can kill plant and animal life and can make drinking water unsafe.

205

The water most people use goes down a drain, through pipes and tunnels, to a place where it is cleaned.

A screen stops big pieces of waste.

Water moves slowly in a tank, so pieces of waste sink to the bottom.

The water moves even more slowly in the next tank. Smaller bits of waste sink to the bottom.

People use water for many things, for cooking, washing, or drinking. No matter what we use it for, it becomes waste water and has to be cleaned before we can reuse it in our homes. Notice the pipe on the diagram above that carries waste water from a house. Some communities do not clean their waste. They may empty waste water directly into lakes, rivers, or the ocean.

Waste can also pollute the soil. If people don't get rid of home or factory wastes properly, the harmful chemicals can leak into the ground and poison our soil. ■

■ What are some of the causes of pollution?

What We Can Do

The problems of air, water, and soil pollution are not easy to solve. Many people are trying to find answers.

Scientists are working on ways to cut back air pollution. They are inventing new car engines and new types of fuel that produce cleaner air.

There are ways for factories to make less air pollution. Some harmful materials can be replaced with less harmful ones. Factories that must use dangerous materials can use filters. Filters are like nets. They can catch the poisons before they get into the air. ■

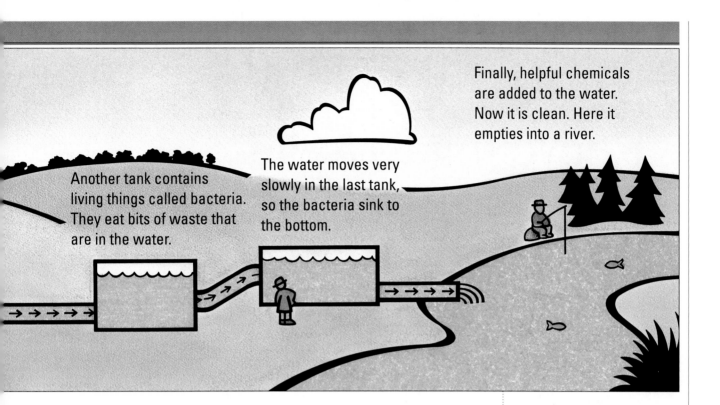

Another tank contains living things called bacteria. They eat bits of waste that are in the water.

The water moves very slowly in the last tank, so the bacteria sink to the bottom.

Finally, helpful chemicals are added to the water. Now it is clean. Here it empties into a river.

Communities and factories can also help stop water pollution. They can stop pouring waste water into lakes, rivers, and oceans. As the diagram shows, waste water needs to be cleaned before it is put back into nature, just as it is cleaned before we can use it again at home.

Dangerous wastes from communities and factories don't have to be dumped on the ground. They can be destroyed, made harmless, or cleaned and used again. If they must be stored underground, they can be sealed in special boxes, so they don't leak into the soil.

You can help solve pollution problems, too. You can encourage your family to walk instead of using the car when it is possible. You may choose to write to people who make laws and tell them to work for clean air and water. What other ways can you think of? ■

■ *What can we do to cut down on soil, water, and air pollution?*

R E V I E W

1. **FOCUS** Why is it important to lower the amount of pollution?
2. **CONNECT** Some problems can be caused by chemicals used in farming and by smoke from steel mills. What natural resources can these pollute?
3. **CRITICAL THINKING** Think of three ways that you can get people more interested in pollution.
4. **ACTIVITY** Make posters that show ways people can lower pollution. Display them for others to see.

Recycling to Save Our Resources

Key Terms

- decompose
- recycling

In March of 1987, this boat left New York. It was taking a load of garbage to North Carolina. When the boat arrived in North Carolina, however, it was not allowed to unload. The people there would not take the garbage.

The boat left North Carolina and went to ports in other states and in other countries to try to get rid of its load. The people in these places would not take the garbage either. Finally, after months of traveling from place to place, the boat returned to New York where the garbage was burned.

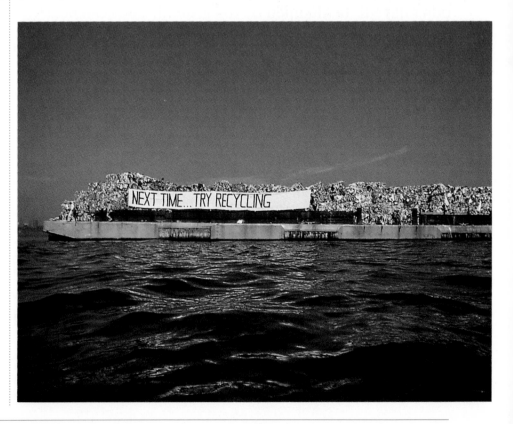

The Garbage Problem

Some people say that by the year 2000, each person in the United States will throw away about six pounds of garbage a day. Why will we have so much garbage? Half of our garbage is packages that hold items we buy and use.

Think about your garbage. Do you throw away a lot of packages? Americans expect products they buy to be well wrapped. Toothpaste, for example, comes in a plastic tube *and* a cardboard container. Crackers are wrapped in plastic *and* put in a cardboard box. When we use the products, we throw the packages away. We must have a place to put this garbage.

Some of our packages harm the environment because they **decompose,** or rot, very slowly. Plastic, metal, and glass, for example, take many years to decompose. People are trying to find ways of solving the problem. ■

■ *What makes up much of our garbage?*

◄ *These children are doing their part to help the environment. What can you and your friends do?*

Recycling

We throw away so much garbage that we are running out of places to dump it all. How can we throw away less garbage? One way is to turn it into something new that can be used again. This is called **recycling.**

The United States recycles about 10% of its trash.

Western Europe recycles about 30%.

Japan recycles about 50%.

Wouldn't it be great if we could recycle all our trash?

▲ *What are some ways to encourage people in the United States to recycle their garbage?*

■ *Why is recycling important?*

▼ *This chart shows that much of the waste in U.S. homes is made up of materials that can be recycled.*

Some garbage can be recycled into things we need. Old newspapers can be made into new paper or building materials. Plastic bottles can be made into other plastic products. Glass can be made into new glass. Aluminum cans can be made into new cans. These materials and others can be recycled and used again. Recycling helps us make less garbage. ■

You Can Help

Protecting the environment is a big job, but we can all do our part. Planning ahead is a good way to start. We can carefully think about what products to buy before we buy them. This will help us plan what to do with our garbage.

Many communities have recycling centers. Is there a center where you live? If so, can you think of ways to recycle the garbage from your own home? Maybe you could start by sorting your garbage. You could separate cans, plastic, paper, and glass from the rest of your family's garbage. Then take these items to the recycling center. From there, your garbage will be shipped to places where it can be made into new products.

Waste in U.S. Homes

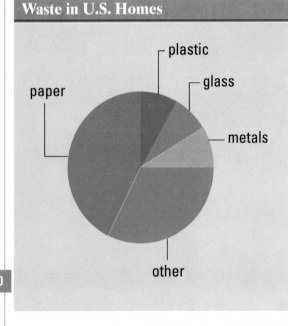

plastic

glass

paper

metals

other

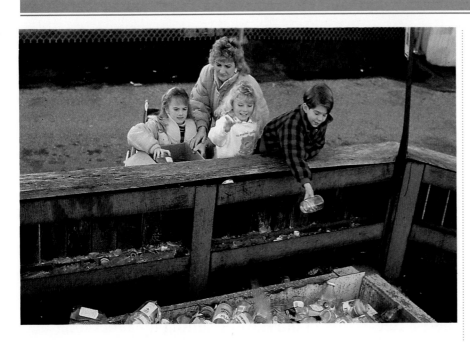

Recycling centers like this one help us to use much of our trash again.

Does your school have a recycling program? If not, can you think of ways to get one started?

Many communities also have programs to make it easy for people to recycle. For example, in some areas people are given containers in which to place newspapers, plastics, and glass. Then on certain days, trucks pick up these items at people's homes.

If you live in an area that does not have a recycling program or recycling centers, there is still something you can do to help protect our natural resources. You may want to write letters to lawmakers and ask them to try to bring recycling centers to your area. You can ask your teacher to give you the names and addresses of the people who make the laws where you live.

Each year, more and more people are becoming interested in recycling. We all must work together to conserve our resources. ■

Across Time & Space

Pioneers recycled things that many of us throw away today. For example, they made old clothing into quilts and used cooking grease to make soap or medicine.

■ *How can people help solve our trash problem?*

R E V I E W

1. **FOCUS** How does recycling help to make our garbage problem smaller?
2. **CONNECT** How can conservation and recycling help us protect our forest land?
3. **CRITICAL THINKING** Why is it important that people start to recycle their garbage now?
4. **ACTIVITY** Make something useful from an empty package. For example, a juice can can be made into a pencil holder. Share your idea with friends.

Recycling Products

Here's Why You have seen how important recycling is to our environment. Recycling helps to save our natural resources. It also helps solve the problem of getting rid of trash.

Suppose you wanted to recycle products. Where would you start?

Here's How You could start by setting up a recycling center in your school or classroom. Your class can work together on the project.

First, decide on the products you are going to recycle. Choose paper, glass, aluminum, plastics, or any combination of products. Then divide your class into small groups. Each group can collect one kind of trash.

Find containers for each type of trash you plan to recycle. If you use plastic bags, be sure they are the kind that can be recycled. The box they come in will tell you if they can be recycled.

You might want to have a theme for your recycling center. Work in groups to draw pictures and make up names for "monsters" that might eat a particular type of waste. For example, children in Toledo, Ohio, feed their glass bottles into the mouth of "Chewbottle." Aluminum cans go into a crusher named "Jaws."

Try It Each day for a week, pick up trash around your school. Put each kind of trash into its recycling container. Do not mix different kinds of trash in one container. At the end of the week, arrange to have the trash taken to a community recycling center.

Apply It Set up a recycling center in your home. Work with your family to recycle paper, cans, and other trash. Put each kind of trash in its own container. Help your family take the trash to a community recycling center.

Chapter Review

Reviewing Key Terms

conservation (p. 199)   recycling (p.209)
decompose (p. 209)   topsoil (p. 199)
environment (p. 203)   waste (p. 205)
pollution (p. 205)

A. Write the key term that best completes each sentence.

1. Harmful chemicals and waste in the air, water, or soil cause _____.
2. Some plastic bags may hurt our environment because they do not _____ easily.
3. _____ is blown away in a windstorm when there are no plants to hold it in place.
4. Turning garbage into something that can be used again is called _____.
5. _____ is taking good care of our natural resources.
6. Trash, garbage, and things we often throw away are _____.
7. Our _____ is the air, water, and land around us.

Exploring Concepts

A. The chart below shows some of the many things we throw away. Copy the chart. In the second column, list one or more ways that each thing can be recycled. Try to think of some ideas of your own for ways to recycle.

B. Write one or two sentences to answer each question.

1. What can farmers do to keep from losing topsoil in dust storms?
2. What are some of the things that cause pollution?

Things we throw away	Ways to recycle
Plastic forks	
Metal cans	
Newspapers	
Glass jars	

Reviewing Skills

1. Sometimes you outgrow your clothes and they no longer fit. For a group project, bring some of your outgrown clothes to school. Sort and fold the clothes. Then put them in paper bags. Give your clothes to a group or an organization that gives clothing to people who need it.

2. Write two "If . . . then" statements that tell what might happen if more people learn about the problems of pollution.

Using Critical Thinking

1. What might happen in our cities if we do not try to reduce air pollution?

2. Farmers use chemicals to make crops grow better and to kill insects that eat plants. Do you think the use of such chemicals is good or bad? Why?

3. If we had no national parks, what would our country be like?

Preparing for Citizenship

1. **ART ACTIVITY** Work in small groups. Use waste materials such as plastics, packaging, newspaper, and string to make a model of a national park.

2. **COLLABORATIVE LEARNING** Have a class trial for someone who is accused of throwing trash in the park. Choose a judge, twelve jury members, witnesses, and the person who is accused of the crime. Have the witnesses tell the judge why they think the person is innocent or guilty. Then, the jury should meet and decide if the accused person is innocent or guilty. If the accused person is guilty, the jury should decide what the punishment will be.

Chapter 11

Our Holidays and Symbols

We the people of the United States of America are proud of our country. We set aside holidays that celebrate important events from our history and honor special people. We choose symbols that remind us that we are a nation of people who are free and proud of our land.

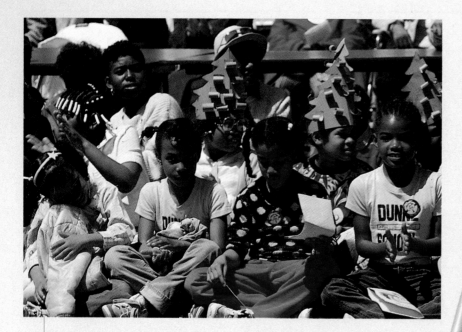

These children are celebrating Arbor Day by wearing evergreen tree hats. On this day we plant trees to show our pride in the beauty of the land.

The flag is a national symbol that shows some of the history of our nation. Each stripe stands for one of the first 13 colonies. The 50 stars stand for the 50 states that today make up the United States.

The bald eagle is also a symbol of the United States. This strong, proud bird shows our courage, our respect for the land, and our love of freedom.

The Washington Monument is a national symbol that honors George Washington, our first president. It stands in our country's capital, Washington, D.C.

Celebrating Our Land

Johnny Appleseed

Of Jonathan Chapman
Two things are known,
That he loved apples,
That he walked alone.

For fifty years over
Of harvest and dew,
He planted his apples
Where no apples grew.

Why did he do it?
We do not know.
He wished that apples
might root and grow.

Rosemary Carr and Stephen Vincent Benet

Arbor Day

Many poems and tales have been written about Johnny Appleseed. Most of these are a mix of truth and imagination. The stories are based on a real man named John Chapman. He lived during the late 1700s and early 1800s. For forty years, he traveled from Pennsylvania to Illinois planting apple trees.

Few apple trees grew where John Chapman traveled so he planted apple trees from the East as he went. He would also give apple trees and apple seeds to settlers he met. People began to call him Johnny Appleseed.

◄ Settlers said that Johnny Appleseed traveled barefooted through the wilderness giving apple seeds or small apple trees to every person he met along the way.

Across Time & Space

J. Sterling Morton's Arbor Day was not the first time trees were planted on a special day. Hundreds of years ago, a group of people that lived in Mexico planted a tree whenever a child was born.

Some people remember Johnny Appleseed and his trees on Arbor Day. This is a holiday that is set aside for planting trees. It is called Arbor Day because an arbor is a place that is shaded by trees.

Arbor Day was started by J. Sterling Morton, who worked with lawmakers in Nebraska. Because Nebraska is part of the dry plains of the United States, few trees grow there naturally. Morton saw that trees were needed to provide wood for the people who were moving to Nebraska. Trees would also protect the land. The plains received very little rain. Tree roots would help keep the soil in place and hold water. They would also slow the wind during dust storms and snow storms.

◄ Today some people in the United States celebrate Arbor Day by planting trees.

This 1932 painting by Grant Wood is called Arbor Day. *It shows a teacher and students planting a tree in front of their school on Arbor Day.*

■ *On Arbor Day, how do people show that they care for the land?*

J. Sterling Morton planned a tree-planting day. That day, April 10, 1872, was the first Arbor Day. The whole state of Nebraska celebrated by planting trees. As news of Arbor Day spread, more and more states began to celebrate this special day.

Arbor Day is still a holiday in Nebraska, though it is now celebrated on April 22. This day was Morton's birthday. Different states celebrate this holiday on different days of the year, but it is celebrated throughout most of the United States and in some parts of Canada. Other countries also set aside days and even weeks as a time to plant trees.

Celebrating Arbor Day gives people the chance to give back to the land some of the things that are taken from it. It also reminds us that it is important to protect our natural resources, especially the land. ■

National Holidays

Arbor Day became a Nebraska holiday when lawmakers there decided the state would celebrate it each year. Other states celebrate Arbor Day, too. In the United States, each state can choose different holidays that its citizens will celebrate.

Some holidays are celebrated by every state in our country. Holidays that are called by the national government and that honor our country and its people are called **national holidays.** The chart on this page shows some of the national holidays that we celebrate.

National Holidays		
Holiday	**Date**	**What We Honor**
Martin L. King, Jr., Day	Third Monday in January	Martin L. King, Jr.'s, birthday
Presidents' Day	Third Monday in February	George Washington's and Abraham Lincoln's birthdays
Memorial Day	Last Monday in May	U.S. soldiers killed in war
Independence Day	July 4	Independence from England
Labor Day	First Monday in September	Working people
Columbus Day	Second Monday in October	European discovery of America
Veterans' Day	November 11	U.S. soldiers who fought in wars
Thanksgiving Day	Fourth Thursday in November	Pilgrims' first harvest

Some national holidays celebrate famous events in history. On Thanksgiving Day, for example, we remember how the Pilgrims thanked God for their harvest and celebrated with the Wampanoag, who had helped them. On Independence Day, we remember July 4, 1776, the day early leaders of America stated that the United States was free from England. Today on July 4, we also celebrate the freedoms that American citizens have. Each year, new citizens, like the one on the next page, join the United States to enjoy the rights and freedoms of our country.

An Immigrant on July 4

1:15 P.M., July 4, 1991
At an Independence Day parade
in Corpus Christi, Texas

Flag
This young immigrant happily tells everyone she meets that she is now a citizen of the United States. Waving the flag is another way for her to say that she is proud of her new country.

Lone Star Button
For her, living in the United States also means living in Texas. This button shows a star, the symbol of Texas. She plans to pin it on her uncle when he moves to the United States next year.

Camera
The pictures she takes of today's celebration will be a wonderful surprise for her friend Tina in Guatemala. The two girls write to each other each week. Tina hopes to visit the United States someday.

Purse
She was given this purse for her ninth birthday. The colorful Guatemalan fabric was woven by hand by her grandmother.

Two of our national holidays honor well-known citizens of our country. We honor George Washington and Abraham Lincoln on Presidents' Day. On Martin Luther King, Jr., Day, we remember this man who fought for freedom for all people.

Some national holidays honor many of our citizens. On Labor Day, we honor all people who work, or labor, to provide things we need. On Veterans' Day, we remember Americans who have fought to keep our country free. Memorial Day is a holiday when we remember soldiers who have died during wars. All of these holidays remind us of the ideas and the beliefs that make our land great. ■

■ *What kinds of people and events do our national holidays celebrate?*

◄ *For many people national holidays are a time to remember our country and all that it gives us.*

R E V I E W

1. **FOCUS** Why do Americans celebrate state and national holidays?
2. **CONNECT** How do stories about men like Johnny Appleseed and Joe Magarac help us remember good things about our country?
3. **CRITICAL THINKING** Think of a person or an event that is important enough to be honored as a national holiday. Write a paragraph telling why.
4. **ACTIVITY** Choose two holidays that you know. Draw a picture that shows what we honor on these days. Make a holiday book that contains your picture and your classmates' pictures.

▼ The Liberty Bell has been cracked twice. It hasn't been rung since 1835, the second time it broke.

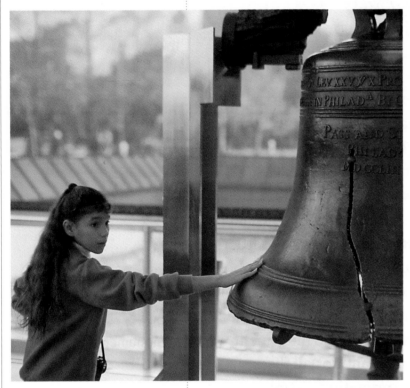

Different nations use different symbols to show their feelings about themselves and their land. We Americans pick national symbols that stand for what is special about our country. Our symbols stand for our pride and good feelings about the United States.

For example, the Liberty Bell is a symbol of the **liberty,** or freedom, that Americans believe in. The Liberty Bell was rung in 1776 when the United States declared its independence from England. Today it hangs in Philadelphia, Pennsylvania.

Other cities have monuments that are national symbols. A **monument** is a building that honors a person or an event. If you were to visit our nation's capital, Washington, D.C., you could see the tall Washington Monument. It was built to honor George Washington. The Gateway Arch stands west of the Mississippi River in St. Louis, Missouri. This stainless steel monument honors the pioneers who moved West to settle the land.

Preserving Our Symbols

These symbols are special because they remind us of important ideas and beliefs about our country and our land. That is why we should try to preserve them.

Today the bald eagle is so rare that it is in danger of dying out. Pollution and hunting have put the bald eagle in danger. Changes to the land have made it hard for the eagle to find food to eat and places to build nests.

How Do We Know?

How do we know that eagles are in danger? The U.S. Fish and Wildlife Service sends out teams of people to study bald eagles and keep track of how many new ones are born each year. The teams usually watch the birds with binoculars from a distance. That way, the eagles aren't frightened.

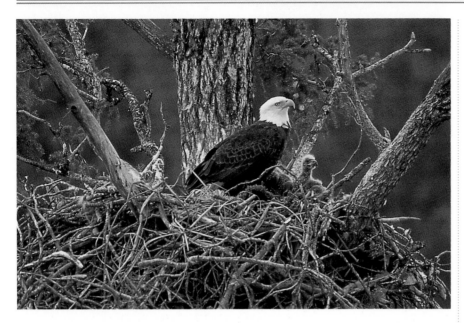

An important reason the bald eagle was chosen as a national symbol was that it lived only in North America. The bald eagle has been seen in each of the United States, except Hawaii.

If we work together to care for bald eagles, however, we can help them become plentiful again. As long as they are not hunted and have trees, clean food, and clean land to live on, they will be safe. ■

■ *Why is the eagle a good symbol of the United States?*

Old Glory

The best-known symbol of the United States is our flag. Sometimes it is called "Old Glory." The flag is a symbol of the idea that we are one nation made up of separate states.

Look at the flag on this stamp. It has 50 stars. Each star stands for one state in our country. The 50 stars mean our nation has 50 states. Our flag also has 13 stripes. Each stripe stands for one of the 13 English colonies that were settled in America.

Our flag is a symbol both of our history and of our nation today, but it has not always looked as it does now. The postage stamps we use to mail letters all over the country have shown a history of our flag. On the next page you can see some of the forms our flag has taken.

This 1988 stamp shows "Old Glory" as it looks today. The U.S. Postal Service makes sure that it has an up-to-date flag stamp at all times.

▼ *What is wrong with this can of asparagus? It's against the law to use the flag to advertise or sell products.*

227

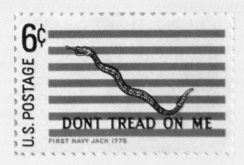

This 1775 flag shows a snake warning enemies not to tread, or step, on it. It was the first flag to be flown on U.S. Navy ships.

The first Congress decided to use this flag in 1777. Its 13 stripes and stars stand for the original colonies and states. This flag is called the "Stars and Stripes."

This flag is the "Star Spangled Banner." Our national anthem was written about this flag with 15 stars and stripes. It was our country's flag from 1795 to 1818.

In 1959 the flag had 48 stars, as this one does. Two more stars were added later that year when Alaska and Hawaii became our 49th and 50th states.

How does the flag symbolize our history, as well as our nation today?

As you can see, the flag has changed from the time before we won our independence from England to today. As states joined the union, stars were added to the flag. Whatever form the flag took, it has always stood for a single nation that believes in "liberty and justice for all." ■

R E V I E W

1. **FOCUS** Why do we have national symbols?

2. **CONNECT** How was the flag changed as our nation moved West?

3. **CRITICAL THINKING** Name other things that might be used as a national symbol.

4. **ACTIVITY** Create your own flag. Choose designs that remind you of the land and people that you learned about in this book. Let these be the symbols on your flag. Display and discuss your design with your classmates.

Chapter Review

Reviewing Key Terms

liberty (p. 226)
national holiday (p. 221)
monument (p. 226)

A. Write *true* or *false* for each sentence. If a sentence is false, rewrite it to make it true.

1. A national holiday celebrates a famous event in our history or honors people of our country.
2. A place to hold indoor games is called a monument.

3. Liberty is freedom from control by others.

B. Write the correct key term for each numbered blank.

Presidents' Day is a __1__ when people throughout the country honor the past presidents of the United States. In Washington, D.C., people may visit a __2__ that honors Abraham Lincoln. Our presidents must work for __3__ and justice for all.

Exploring Concepts

A. The bald eagle is our national symbol. Copy the chart. Fill in the second column to show what the early Indians might have chosen for their symbols.

B. Long ago the bald eagle was chosen to be our national symbol. Write two reasons why you think that was a good choice.

Indian people	Symbol
Kwakiutl	
Cheyenne	
Navajo	

Reviewing Skills

1. Read the second paragraph on page 219 again. In one or two sentences, write a summary of the paragraph in your own words.

2. Draw a map to show that Johnny Appleseed walked ten miles in one day from one town to another. Use a scale of one inch for one mile.

Using Critical Thinking

1. The Wampanoag and the Delaware helped the Pilgrims and the early settlers survive in the wilderness. Do you think monuments should be built in their honor? If so, where?

2. The picture shows children planting trees on Arbor Day many years ago. Today, some towns celebrate Arbor Day and hold tree-planting ceremonies. Do you think Arbor Day should be a national holiday? Why?

Preparing for Citizenship

1. **ART ACTIVITY** The Liberty Bell is a symbol of our liberty and freedom. Draw a picture of something else that you think would be a good symbol of our liberty. Show your picture to the class. Tell them why it is a good symbol of liberty.

2. **COLLABORATIVE LEARNING** Divide the class into four groups. Each group should prepare a short skit, song, or poem about someone who did something special for our country. Perform your skits, songs, or poems for other classes in your school.

Time/Space Databank

WORLD: *Political*

ABBREVIATIONS

CEN. AFR. REP.
    Central African Republic
DEN. Denmark
FR. France
GR. Greece
IT. Italy
N. North, Northern
NETH. Netherlands
P.D.R. YEMEN
    People's Democratic
    Republic of Yemen
PORT. Portugal
S. South
SP. Spain
TERR. Territory
U.A.E. United Arab
    Emirates
U.K. United Kingdom
U.S. United States
W. Western

— National boundary

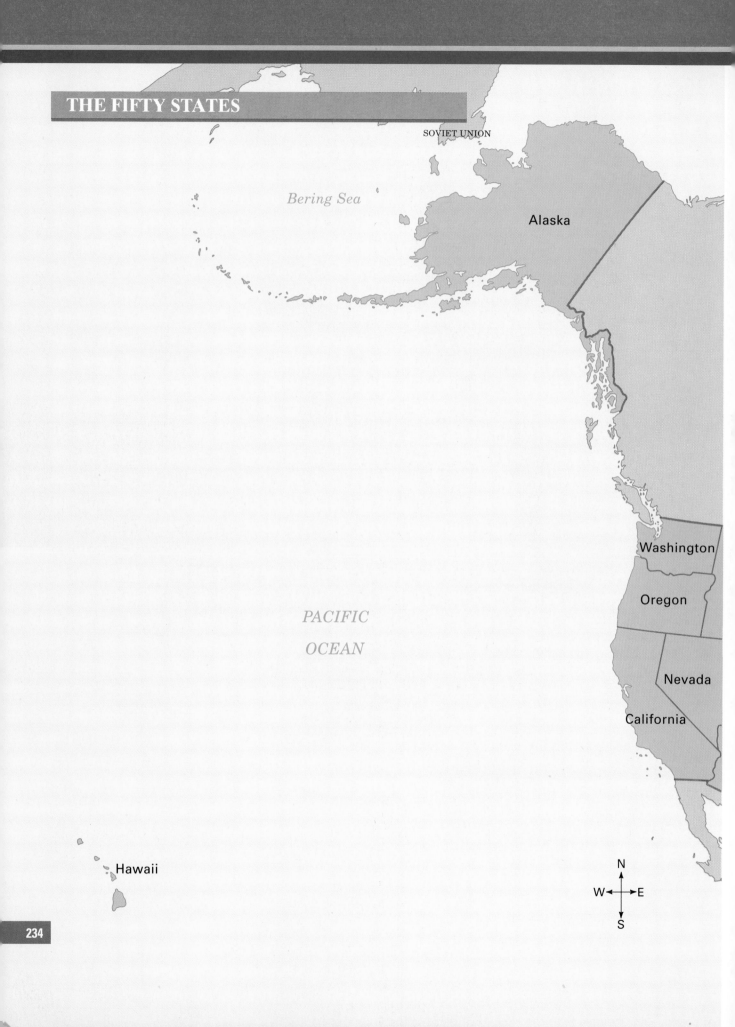

SOVIET UNION

Bering Sea

Alaska

PACIFIC

OCEAN

Washington

Oregon

Nevada

California

Hawaii

N
W ←→ E
S

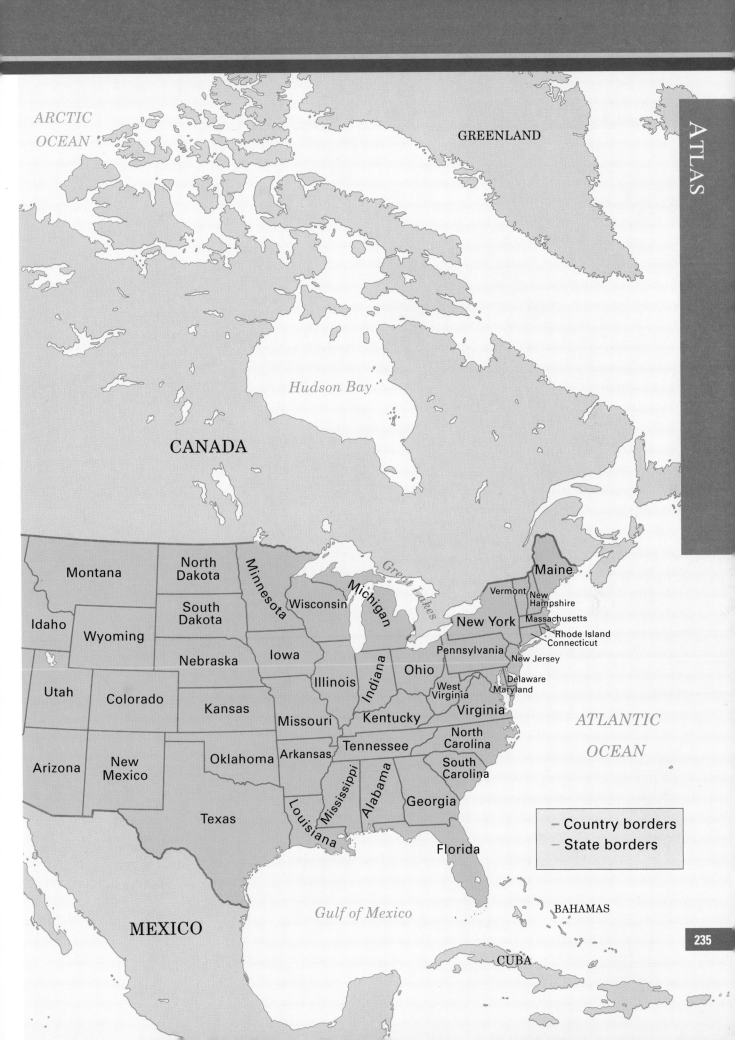

ARCTIC
OCEAN

GREENLAND

Hudson Bay

CANADA

Montana

North
Dakota

Minnesota

Great Lakes

Michigan

Maine

Idaho

Wyoming

South
Dakota

Wisconsin

Vermont
New
Hampshire

New York

Massachusetts

Utah

Nebraska

Iowa

Illinois

Indiana

Ohio

Pennsylvania

Rhode Island
Connecticut

New Jersey

Colorado

Kansas

Missouri

Kentucky

West
Virginia

Delaware
Maryland

Virginia

ATLANTIC

Arizona

New
Mexico

Oklahoma

Arkansas

Tennessee

North
Carolina

OCEAN

Texas

Louisiana

Mississippi

Alabama

South
Carolina

Georgia

Florida

— Country borders
— State borders

MEXICO

Gulf of Mexico

BAHAMAS

235

CUBA

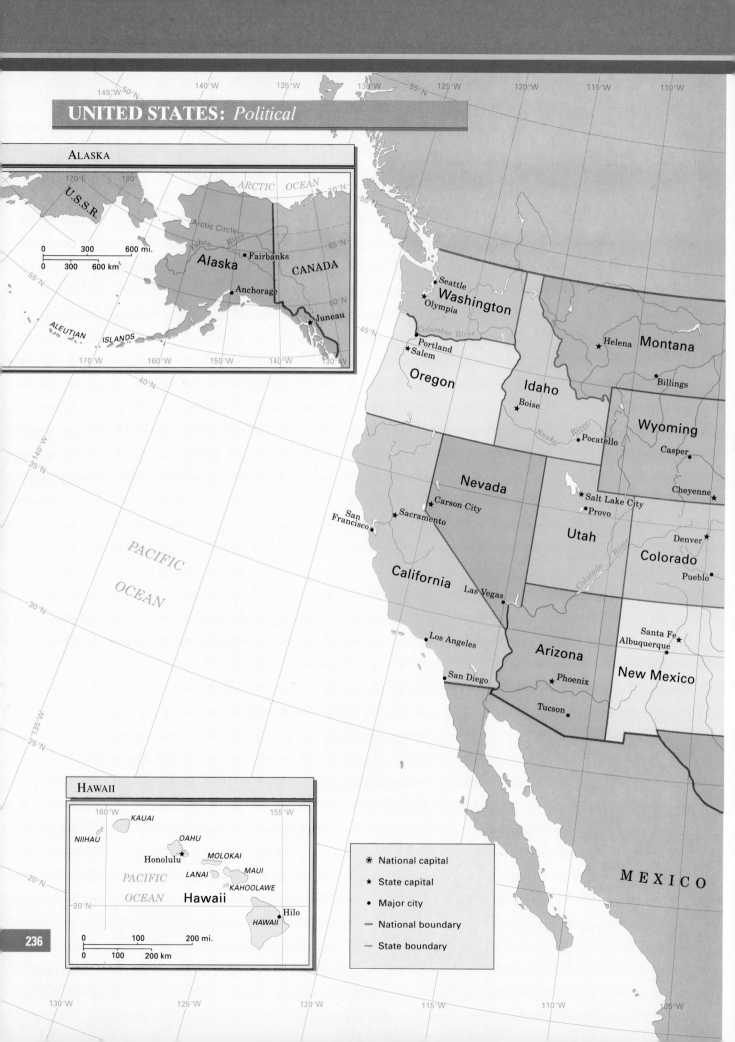

UNITED STATES: *Political*

ALASKA

U.S.S.R.

ARCTIC OCEAN

Arctic Circle

Yukon River

Alaska
• Fairbanks

CANADA

• Anchorage

• Juneau

ALEUTIAN ISLANDS

170°E 180 170°W 160°W 150°W 140°W 130°W
50°N 65°N 60°N 55°N

0   300   600 mi.
0   300   600 km

PACIFIC

OCEAN

ARCTIC OCEAN

Seattle
Washington
Olympia

Columbia River
Portland
★ Salem

Oregon

Helena
Montana

• Billings

Idaho
Boise ★

Shake River

• Pocatello

Wyoming

• Casper

Cheyenne ★

Nevada

★ Carson City
• Sacramento

San Francisco

★ Salt Lake City
• Provo

Utah

Colorado River

Denver ★

Colorado

• Pueblo

California

Las Vegas

• Los Angeles

• San Diego

Arizona

• Phoenix ★

Tucson •

Santa Fe ★
Albuquerque •

New Mexico

HAWAII

KAUAI
NIIHAU
OAHU
Honolulu ★
MOLOKAI
LANAI MAUI
KAHOOLAWE

PACIFIC

OCEAN
Hawaii
HAWAII
Hilo •

160°W 155°W
20°N

0   100   200 mi.
0   100   200 km

MEXICO

⊛ National capital

★ State capital

• Major city

〰 National boundary

— State boundary

236

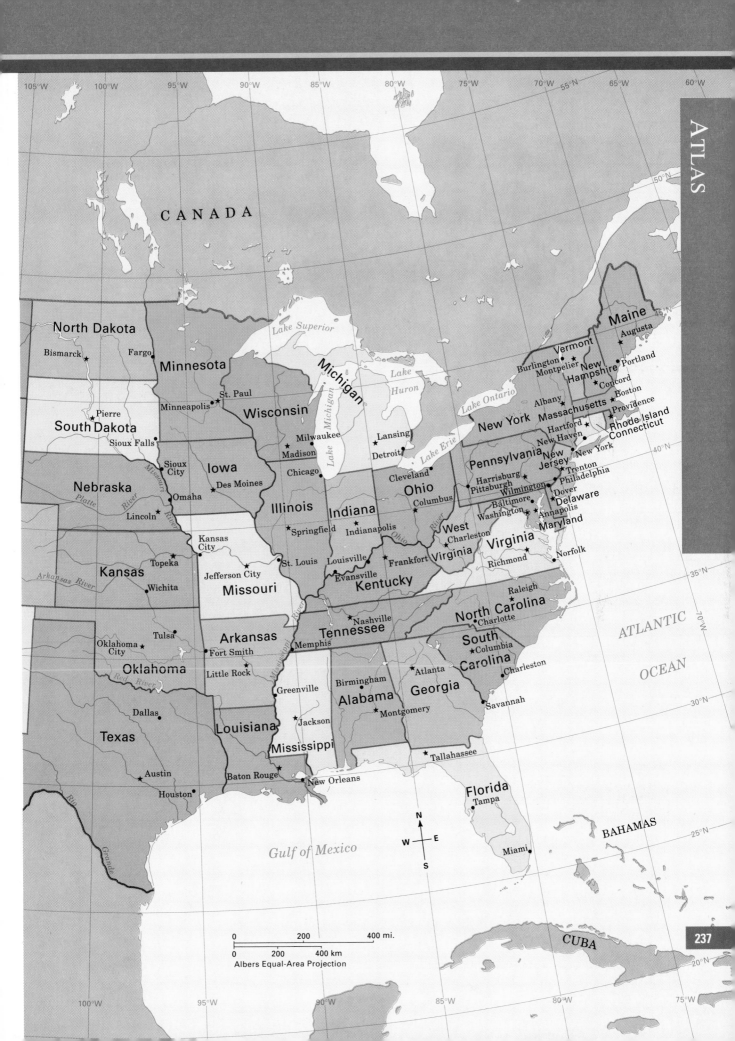

105°W · 100°W · 95°W · 90°W · 85°W · 80°W · 75°W · 70°W · 55°N · 65°W · 60°W

CANADA

Lake Superior

North Dakota

Bismarck • Fargo •

Minnesota

Lake Huron

Michigan

50°N

Vermont
Maine

Augusta

Burlington • Montpelier New Portland
Hampshire

Concord

Boston

Lake Michigan

Madison

Lansing

Lake Erie

Lake Ontario

Albany

New York

Massachusetts
Providence

Pierre •

South Dakota

Sioux Falls •

St. Paul

Wisconsin

Minneapolis •

Milwaukee •

Detroit •

Hartford
Rhode Island
New Haven Connecticut

Sioux
City •

Iowa

Chicago •

Cleveland •

Ohio

Pennsylvania
New
Jersey
New York

40°N

Nebraska

Des Moines •

Harrisburg
Pittsburgh •

Trenton

Philadelphia

Lincoln •

Omaha •

Illinois

Indiana

Wilmington

Dover

Platte

River

Missouri

River

Springfield •

Indianapolis •

Ohio

Columbus •

Baltimore •
Washington •

Delaware

Annapolis
Maryland

Kansas
City •

St. Louis •

Louisville •

Frankfort •

West
Charleston
Virginia

Virginia

Richmond •

Kansas

Topeka •

Jefferson City •

Evansville •

River

Kentucky

Norfolk •

35°N

Arkansas River

Wichita •

Missouri

Raleigh •

70°W

Oklahoma
City •

Tulsa •

Arkansas

Nashville •

Tennessee

Memphis •

North Carolina
Charlotte •

ATLANTIC

Oklahoma

Fort Smith •

South
★ Columbia
Carolina

OCEAN

Red River

Little Rock •

Greenville •

Birmingham •

Atlanta •

Georgia

Charleston •

30°N

Dallas •

Louisiana

Jackson •

Alabama

Montgomery •

Savannah •

Texas

Austin •

Mississippi

Baton Rouge •

New Orleans •

Tallahassee •

25°N

Houston •

Rio Grande

N
W E
S

Gulf of Mexico

Florida

Tampa •

BAHAMAS

Miami •

Albers Equal-Area Projection

0 · 200 · 400 mi.

0 · 200 · 400 km

CUBA

20°N

100°W · 95°W · 90°W · 85°W · 80°W · 75°W

UNITED STATES: *Physical*

ALASKA

U.S.S.R.

ARCTIC OCEAN

BROOKS RANGE

SEWARD PEN.

Arctic Circle

CANADA

Mt. McKinley
20,320 ft.
6,194 m

ALASKA RANGE

ALEUTIAN ISLANDS

KODIAK

0   300   600 mi.
0   300   600 km

PACIFIC
OCEAN

CANADA

COASTAL RANGE

CASCADE RANGE

Mt. Rainier
14,410 ft.
4,392 m

Mt. St. Helens
8,364 ft.
2,549 m

Mt. Hood
11,239 ft.
3,426 m

COLUMBIA PLATEAU

BITTERROOT RANGE

R O C K Y   M O U N T A I N S

Missouri River

Yellowstone River

BIG HORN MTS.

Mt. Shasta
14,162 ft.
4,317 m

COASTAL RANGES

SIERRA NEVADA

CENTRAL VALLEY

GREAT BASIN

Great Salt Lake

Snake River

WASATCH RANGE

UINTA MTS.

CONTINENTAL

Pikes Peak
14,110 ft.
4,310 m

San Francisco Bay

Mt. Whitney
14,494 ft.
4,418 m

DEATH VALLEY

MOJAVE DESERT

GRAND CANYON

PAINTED DESERT

Colorado River

DIVIDE

SANGRE DE CRISTO MTS.

CHANNEL ISLANDS

Colorado River

Gila River

Rio Grande

SACRAMENTO MTS.

Pecos River

MEXICO

HAWAIIAN ISLANDS

KAUAI

NIIHAU

OAHU

MOLOKAI

LANAI   MAUI

KAHOOLAWE

PACIFIC
OCEAN

HAWAII

0   100   200 mi.
0   100   200 km

Land Elevation

Feet	Meters
13,120	4,000
6,560	2,000
1,640	500
656	200
0	0
Below sea level	Below sea level

Ice-covered land

▲ Mountain Peak

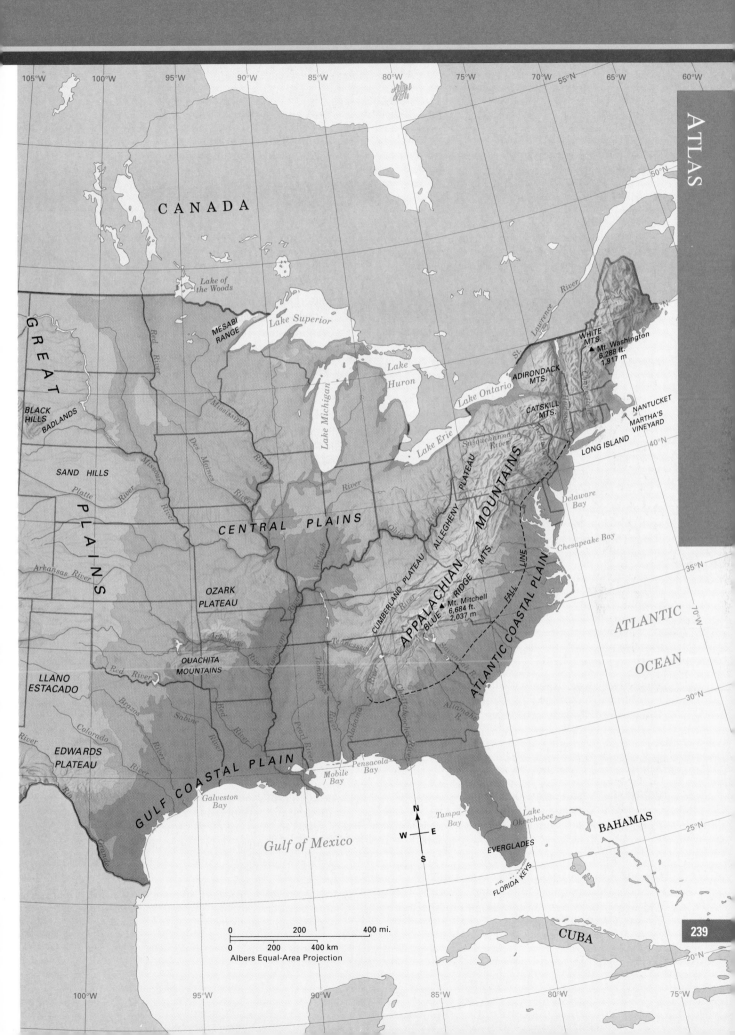

105°W 100°W 95°W 90°W 85°W 80°W 75°W 70°W 55°N 65°W 60°W

50°N

CANADA

Lake of
the Woods

MESABI
RANGE

Lake Superior

Lake Michigan

Lake Huron

Lake Ontario

Lake Erie

St. Lawrence River

WHITE
MTS.

Mt. Washington
6,288 ft.
1,917 m

ADIRONDACK
MTS.

CATSKILL
MTS.

NANTUCKET

MARTHA'S
VINEYARD

LONG ISLAND

40°N

GREAT
PLAINS

BLACK
HILLS
BADLANDS

SAND HILLS

Red River

Missouri River

Platte River

Arkansas River

Mississippi River

Des Moines River

River

CENTRAL PLAINS

OZARK
PLATEAU

Ohio River

Wabash River

ALLEGHENY PLATEAU

PLATEAU

Susquehanna River

APPALACHIAN MOUNTAINS

Delaware Bay

Chesapeake Bay

35°N

70°W

LLANO
ESTACADO

EDWARDS
PLATEAU

OUACHITA
MOUNTAINS

Red River

Arkansas River

CUMBERLAND PLATEAU

BLUE RIDGE MTS.

Mt. Mitchell
6,684 ft.
2,037 m

Tennessee River

FALL LINE

ATLANTIC COASTAL PLAIN

ATLANTIC

OCEAN

30°N

Colorado River

Brazos River

Sabine River

Red River

Pearl River

Tombigbee River

Alabama River

Chattahoochee R.

Savannah R.

Altamaha R.

GULF COASTAL PLAIN

Rio Grande

Galveston
Bay

Mobile
Bay

Pensacola
Bay

Tampa
Bay

Lake
Okeechobee

EVERGLADES

BAHAMAS

25°N

N
W   E
S

Gulf of Mexico

FLORIDA KEYS

CUBA

20°N

0   200   400 mi.
0   200   400 km
Albers Equal-Area Projection

239

100°W 95°W 90°W 85°W 80°W 75°W

Gazetteer

This gazetteer will help you locate many of the places discussed in this book. The page number tells you where to find each place on a map.

A

Abilene Prairie town in Kansas. It became a booming cattle town in the 1860s. (p. 156)

Africa The earth's second largest continent. It lies between the Atlantic and Indian oceans. (pp. 232–233)

Alabama Southeastern state on the Gulf of Mexico. Its capital is Montgomery. (pp. 236–237)

Alaska State farthest north of all states. Its capital is Juneau. (pp. 236–237)

Allegheny River River in eastern United States. It joins the Monongahela River at Pittsburgh to form the Ohio River. (p. 179)

Appalachian Mountains Mountain range in eastern North America. It extends about 1,600 miles from southern Canada to Alabama. (p. 122)

Arizona Southwestern state on the Mexican border. Its capital is Phoenix. (pp. 236–237)

Arkansas South central state. Its capital is Little Rock. (pp. 236–237)

Asia The earth's largest continent. It is separated from Europe by the Ural Mountains. (pp. 232–233)

Atlantic Ocean The earth's second largest body of water. It borders the eastern coast of the United States. (p. 5)

B

Bakersfield City in south central California at the southern end of the San Joaquin Valley. (p. 171)

Boonesboro Pioneer settlement in central Kentucky. Named after Daniel Boone. (p. 135)

C

California Western state on the Pacific coast. Its capital is Sacramento. (pp. 236–237)

California Trail Southern branch of the Oregon Trail. It was used by pioneers traveling to California. (p. 149)

Canada Country to the north of the United States. Its capital is Ottawa. (pp. 232–233)

Chicago City in northeastern Illinois on the shore of Lake Michigan. (p. 156)

Chisholm Trail Main trail for cattle drives out of Texas in the 1860s. It extended from San Antonio, Texas, to Abilene, Kansas. (p. 156)

Colorado Western state. Its capital is Denver. (pp. 236–237)

Colorado River River in southwestern United States. It begins in the mountains of Colorado and flows into the Gulf of California. (p. 21)

Connecticut Northeastern state. Its capital is Hartford. (pp. 236–237)

Cumberland Gap A pass through the Appalachian Mountains where Kentucky, Virginia, and Tennessee join. (p. 135)

D

Delaware Eastern state on the Atlantic coast. Its capital is Dover. (pp. 236–237)

Denver City in north central Colorado. (pp. 236–237)

Dodge City City in southwestern Kansas. (p. 158)

E

England The southern part of the island of Great Britain. People from England started many colonies in North America. (p. 117)

Europe The earth's second smallest continent. It extends west from the Ural Mountains. (pp. 232–233)

F

Florida Southeastern state on the Atlantic coast. Its capital is Tallahassee. (pp. 236–237)

France Country in western Europe. People from France settled in North America beginning in the 1600s. (p. 233)

G

Georgia Southeastern state on the Atlantic coast. Its capital is Atlanta. (pp. 236–237)

Germany Former country in Europe, now divided into two countries. German people came to settle eastern North America in the early 1700s. (p. 233)

Grand Canyon Canyon of the Colorado River in northwestern Arizona. It is 217 miles long and 4 to 18 miles wide. (p. 20)

Great Lakes Group of five lakes between Canada and the United States, including Lakes Superior, Huron, Erie, Ontario, and Michigan. (p. 49)

Guatemala Country in Central America. (p. 232)

Gulf of Mexico Part of the Atlantic Ocean that borders the southern part of the United States and the eastern part of Mexico. (p. 49)

H

Harrodsburg One of two pioneer towns in central Kentucky (with Boonesboro) at which branches of the Wilderness Trail ended. (p. 135)

Hawaii State and island group in the central Pacific Ocean. Its capital is Honolulu. (pp. 236–237)

Holston River River in northeastern Tennessee and southwestern Virginia. The Wilderness Road began there. (p. 135)

Hudson River River in New York. It begins in the mountains of northern New York and flows into the Atlantic Ocean at New York City. (p. 19)

I

Idaho Northwestern state. Its capital is Boise. (pp. 236–237)

Illinois North central state. Its capital is Springfield. (pp. 236–237)

Independence City in western Missouri. In pioneer days, it was the starting point for travelers using the Oregon and Santa Fe Trails. (p. 149)

Indiana North central state. Its capital is Indianapolis. (pp. 236–237)

Iowa North central state. Its capital is Des Moines. (pp. 236–237)

Ireland Small country in the British Isles. People from Ireland settled in eastern North America in the early 1700s. (p. 233)

K

Kansas Central state. Its capital is Topeka. (pp. 236–237)

Kentucky Southeastern state. Its capital is Frankfort. (pp. 236–237)

Kilauea One of two volcanoes in Hawaii Volcanoes National Park. (p. 201)

L

Lake Ontario One of the five Great Lakes, which lie between the United States and Canada. (p. 49)

Leadville Town in central Colorado. It became a boom town of silver mining during the 1870s. (p. 161)

Los Angeles City in southern California on the Pacific coast. In pioneer days, it became the end of the Santa Fe Trail. (pp. 236–237)

Louisiana Southeastern state on the Gulf of Mexico. Its capital is Baton Rouge. (pp. 236–237)

M

Maine Northeastern state on the Atlantic coast. Its capital is Augusta. pp. (236–237)

Maryland Eastern state on the Atlantic coast. Its capital is Annapolis. (pp. 236–237)

Massachusetts Northeastern state on the Atlantic coast. Its capital is Boston. pp. (236–237)

Mauna Loa One of two volcanoes in Hawaii Volcanoes National Park. (p. 201)

Mexico Country to the south of and bordering the United States. Its capital is Mexico City. (p. 21)

Michigan North central state. Its capital is Lansing. (pp. 236–237)

Minnesota North central state. Its capital is St. Paul. (pp. 236–237)

Mississippi Southern state on the Gulf of Mexico. Its capital is Jackson. (pp. 236–237)

Mississippi River Second longest river in the United States. It begins in northern Minnesota and flows into the Gulf of Mexico at New Orleans. (p. 49)

Missouri Central state. Its capital is Jefferson City. (pp. 236–237)

Missouri River Longest river in the United States. It begins in western Montana and flows into the Mississippi River near St. Louis. (pp. 236–237)

Monongahela River River in eastern United States. It joins the Allegheny River at Pittsburgh to form the Ohio River. (p. 179)

Montana Northwestern state. Its capital is Helena. (pp. 236–237)

Mount McKinley Mountain peak in south central Alaska. It is the highest peak in North America at 20,320 feet. (pp. 238–239)

N

Nebraska North central state in the Great Plains. Its capital is Lincoln. (pp. 236–237)

Nevada Western state. Its capital is Carson City. (pp. 236–237)

New Hampshire Northeastern state on the Atlantic coast. Its capital is Concord. (pp. 236–237)

New Jersey Northeastern state on the Atlantic coast. Its capital is Trenton. (pp. 236–237)

New Mexico Southwestern state on the Mexican border. Its capital is Santa Fe. (pp. 236–237)

New York Northeastern state. Its capital is Albany. (pp. 236–237)

New York City City in New York at the mouth of the Hudson River. It is the largest city in the United States. (p. 122)

North America The third largest continent. It includes the countries of the United States, Canada, Mexico, and those of Central America. (pp. 232–233)

North Carolina Southeastern state on the Atlantic coast. Its capital is Raleigh. (pp. 236–237)

North Dakota North central state. Its capital is Bismarck. (pp. 236–237)

North Pole The most northern point of the earth. (p. 159)

O

Ohio North central state. Its capital is Columbus. (pp. 236–237)

Ohio River River formed in Pennsylvania where the Allegheny and the Monongahela rivers join. It flows into the Mississippi River in Illinois. (p. 179)

Oklahoma Southwestern state. Its capital is Oklahoma City. (pp. 236–237)

Oregon Northwestern state on the Pacific coast. Its capital is Salem. (pp. 236–237)

Oregon Trail Pioneer route from Independence, Missouri, to the West. (p. 149)

P

Pacific Ocean The earth's largest body of water. It borders the western coast of the United States. (p. 5)

Pennsylvania Northeastern state. Its capital is Harrisburg. (pp. 236–237)

Philadelphia City in southeastern Pennsylvania on the Delaware River. (p. 122)

Pittsburgh City in southwestern Pennsylvania at the place where the Allegheny and Monongahela rivers meet to form the Ohio River. (p. 179)

Platte River Most important river in Nebraska. Its two branches begin in the mountains of Colorado. (pp. 236–237)

Plymouth Harbor town in southeastern Massachusetts. (p. 117)

Plymouth Colony Second English settlement in America. It was founded by Pilgrims in 1620. (p. 117)

R

Rhode Island Northeastern state on the Atlantic coast. Its capital is Providence. (pp. 236–237)

Rocky Mountains Longest mountain range in North America. It extends more than 3,000 miles from northern Alaska to northern New Mexico. (pp. 238–239)

S

St. Louis City in eastern Missouri on the Mississippi River. (pp. 236–237)

San Antonio City in southern Texas. It was the beginning of the Chisholm Trail during the 1860s. (p. 156)

San Joaquin Valley Rich farming area in central California. The San Joaquin River runs through this land. (p. 171)

Santa Fe City in north central New Mexico. It is the capital of New Mexico. In pioneer days, it was an important stop on the Santa Fe Trail. (p. 149)

Santa Fe Trail Pioneer route from Independence, Missouri, to Santa Fe, New Mexico. It was extended later to Los Angeles, California. (p. 149)

Scotland Northern part of the island of Great Britain. People from Scotland settled in the eastern part of North America in the early 1700s. (p. 233)

Sonoran Desert Desert in southwestern United States and northwestern Mexico. (p. 52)

South America The earth's fourth largest continent. It lies between the Atlantic Ocean and the Pacific Ocean. (pp. 232–233)

South Carolina Southeastern state on the Atlantic coast. Its capital is Columbia. (pp. 236–237)

South Dakota North central state. Its capital is Pierre. (pp. 236–237)

South Pole The most southern point of the earth. (p. 159)

Spain Country in southwestern Europe. People from Spain came to North America to start colonies. (p. 233)

T

Tennessee Southeastern state. Its capital is Nashville. (pp. 236–237)

Teton Mountains Range of the Rocky Mountains in northwestern Wyoming and southeastern Idaho. Grand Teton is the highest peak in the range. (pp. 238–239)

Texas South central state on the Gulf of Mexico coast. Its capital is Austin. (pp. 236–237)

U

United States Country of central and northwestern North America. It is made up of 50 states. Its capital is Washington, D.C. Its abbreviation is U.S. (pp. 232–233)

Utah Western state. Its capital is Salt Lake City. (pp. 236–237)

V

Vermont Northeastern state. Its capital is Montpelier. (pp. 236–237)

Virginia Southeastern state on the Atlantic coast. Its capital is Richmond. (pp. 236–237)

Virginia Colony First English colony in North America, made up of several settlements. (p. 117)

W

Washington Northwestern state on the Pacific coast. Its capital is Olympia. (pp. 236–237)

Washington, D.C. Eastern city on the Potomac River. It is the capital of the United States. (pp. 236–237)

West Virginia East central state. Its capital is Charleston. (pp. 236–237)

Wichita City in south central Kansas. (p. 158)

Wilderness Road Pioneer road from Virginia to Kentucky through the Cumberland Mountains. Daniel Boone led the men who cut the trail for the road. (p. 135)

Wisconsin North central state. Its capital is Madison. (pp. 236–237)

Wyoming Western state. Its capital is Cheyenne. (pp. 236–237)

Y

Yellowstone National Park Oldest and largest United States national park. Most of it is in northwestern Wyoming. It is famous for its hot springs. (p. 200)

GLOSSARY OF GEOGRAPHIC TERMS

mountain
a steeply raised mass of land, much higher than the surrounding country

ocean
a salty body of water covering a large area of the earth (also, **sea**)

tree line
on a mountain, the area above which no trees grow

mountain range
a row of mountains

valley
low land between hills or mountains

highland
land that is higher than most of the surrounding land

forest
a large area of land where many trees grow

hill
a raised mass of land, smaller than a mountain

prairie
a large, level area of grassland without trees

desert
a dry area where few plants grow

plain
a broad, flat area of land

sea level
the level of the surface
of the ocean

harbor
a protected body of water
where ships can safely stop

coast
the land next to
the ocean

river
a large stream of water that
runs into a lake, ocean, or
another river

bay
part of a lake or ocean extend-
ing into the land

island
a body of land with
water all around it

shore
the land along the edge of a
lake, sea, or ocean

lowland
land that is lower than most
of the surrounding land

lake
a body of water with
land all around it

245

Pronunciation Key

Spellings	Symbol	Spellings	Symbol	Spellings	Symbol
pat	ă	kick, cat, pique	k	thin	th
pay	ā	lid, needle	l	this	*th*
care	âr	mum	m	cut	ŭ
father	ä	no, sudden	n	urge, term, firm,	ûr
bib	b	thing	ng	word, heard	
church	ch	pot, horrid	ŏ	valve	v
deed, milled	d	toe	ō	with	w
pet	ě	caught, paw, for	ô	yes	y
bee	ē	noise	oi	zebra, xylem	z
life, phase, rough	f	took	ŏŏ	vision, pleasure,	zh
gag	g	boot	ōō	garage	
hat	h	out	ou	about, item, edible,	ə
which	hw	pop	p	gallop, circus	
pit	ĭ	roar	r	butter	ər
pie, by	ī	sauce	s		
pier	îr	ship, dish	sh	Primary stress ´	
judge	j	tight, stopped	t	Secondary stress ´	

A

adaptation (ăd´ăp-tā´shən) A change in the way of life of people, animals, or plants in order to fit the surroundings in which they live. (p. 101)

agriculture (ăg´rĭ-kŭl´chər) The business of working the soil, growing crops, and raising livestock. (p. 171)

B

blaze (blāz) To mark a trail by cutting bark from a tree. (p. 136)

boom town (bōōm´ tōun´) A town that grows and becomes wealthy very quickly. (p. 162)

C

cedar (sē´dər) A type of evergreen tree whose wood is often reddish in color. (p. 66)

ceremony (sěr´ə-mō´nē) An act that is performed in honor of an important event. People may sing, dance, tell stories, or make speeches during a ceremony. (p. 72)

chant (chănt) A song that is sung on the same note or on a few notes, often as a form of prayer. (p. 103)

climate (klī´mĭt) The weather, including amount of rain, snow, wind, and the degree of coldness or hotness of an area over a long time. (p. 54)

coast (kōst) The land beside a sea. (p. 5)

colony (kŏl´ə-nē) An area that is settled by people from a faraway country and ruled by that home country. (p. 117)

conservation (kŏn´sûr-vā´shən) The protection or wise use of things found in nature that are useful to people. (p. 199)

D

decompose (dē´kəm-pōz´) To rot or fall apart slowly. (p. 209)

desert (dĕz´ərt) A dry, sandy area that gets very little rain. (p. 51)

E

environment (ĕn-vī´rən-mənt) The surroundings in which animals, people, and plants live. (p. 203)

erosion (ĭ-rō´zhən) The slow wearing away of land. (p. 5)

F

fertilizer (fûr´tl-ī´zēr) Chemicals that are added to soil to make plants grow healthier and more quickly. (p. 172)

flood (flŭd) Water that overflows its banks and covers land that is normally dry. (p. 23)

forest (fôr´ĭst) A large area of land that is covered with trees and other plants. (p. 28)

freight (frāt) Materials that are carried by train, ship, truck, or airplane. (p. 183)

G

goods (go͞odz) Things that people buy and sell. (p. 122)

H

hogan (hō´gän´) A one-room Navajo house made of logs covered with mud. Mud kept hogans warm in summer and cool in winter. (p. 99)

humus (hyo͞o´məs) The brown or black matter that is found in soil and made up of rotting plants or animals. (p. 30)

I

industry (ĭn´də-strē) A business that makes things to sell or that provides services. (p. 179)

inland (ĭn´lənd) Away from the coast. (p. 121)

irrigation (ĭr´ĭ-gā´shən) To bring water to dry land through the use of ditches, canals, or pipes. (p. 172)

L

lake (lāk) A large body of water with land all around it. (p. 19)

liberty (lĭb´ər-tē) Freedom from control by others. (p. 226)

livestock (līv´stŏk´) Animals, such as sheep or horses, that are raised for home use or to be sold. (p. 101)

location (lō-kā´shən) The place where something could be or is found. (p. 179)

long house (lông´ hōus´) A house up to 60 feet long that was used by Eastern and Western North American Indians. This type of house was built with logs that were split into thin boards. (p. 67)

M

mineral (mĭn´ər-əl) A naturally occurring material, such as gold or iron, that is found in the earth. (p. 161)

monument (mŏn´yə-mənt) A statue or building that honors a person or an event. (p. 226)

mountain (mōun´tən) Land that has steep sides and a rounded or pointed peak, and that stands much higher than the land around it. (p. 45)

myth (mĭth) A story that explains something in nature or the beliefs that a group of people share. (p. 87)

N

national holiday (năsh´ə-nəl hŏl´ĭ-dā´) A holiday that is set aside by the national government to honor a country and its people. (p. 221)

natural resource (năch´ər-əl rē´sôrs´) Anything that is found in nature that people can use. (p. 81)

O

ocean (ō´shən) A large body of salt water. Oceans cover much of the earth's surface. The three largest oceans of the world are the Pacific, the Atlantic, and the Indian. The Pacific is the largest of the three. (p. 5)

P

pass (păs) A narrow passage at a low point between mountain peaks. (p. 148)

physical feature (fĭz´ĭ-kəl fē´chər) A natural part of the earth's surface. (p. 45)

pioneer (pī´ə-nîr´) A person who is the first to settle in a wilderness area, leading the way for others to follow. (p. 135)

pollution (pə-lōo´shən) Harmful material that makes the air, water, or soil dirty. (p. 205)

population (pŏp´yə-lā´shən) The number of people that live in an area. (p. 155)

prairie (prâr´ē) A large area of flat or hilly land covered by grasses. (p. 34)

predator (prĕd´ə-tər) An animal that lives by hunting other animals for food. (p. 35)

R

recycling (rē-sī´klĭng) The process of treating trash so that it can be used again. (p. 209)

river (rĭv´ər) A large moving stream of water that flows into an ocean, lake, or other body of water. (p. 18)

S

salmon (săm´ən) A type of fish that usually lives in salt water but swims up a river to lay its eggs. (p. 65)

sand painting (sănd´ pān´tĭng) A picture that is made by Navajo Indians with bits of crushed rock, plants, and other dry materials. A sand painting tells a story about nature and spirits. (p. 104)

services (sûr´vĭs-əz) Businesses that perform work or provide help for people. (p. 181)

steel mills (stēl´ mĭlz´) Factories that make steel. (p. 179)

survive (sər-vīv´) To stay alive. (p. 117)

symbol (sĭm´bəl) Something that stands for something else. (p. 88)

T

temperature (tĕm´pər-ə-choŏr´) The degree of coldness or hotness of something. (p. 45)

timberline (tĭm´bər-līn´) The limit of height on a mountain above which trees do not grow. (p. 45)

tipi (tē´pē) A cone-shaped tent made of animal skins or bark used by some North American Indians. (p. 81)

topsoil (tŏp´soĭl´) The top layer of soil, usually darker and richer than the soil beneath it. (p. 199)

totem pole (tō´təm pōl´) A wooden pole that Northwest Coast Indians decorated with carved figures that may help show a family's history. (p. 71)

trade (trād) The business of buying and selling goods. (p. 184)

trade center (trād´ sĕn´tər) A town or city where people take part in buying and selling goods and services. (p. 156)

transportation (trăns´pər-tā´shən) A system or way of moving passengers or things that people buy and sell. (p. 184)

V

vein (vān) A long strip of mineral found in rock. (p. 160)

W

wagon train (wăg´ən trān´) A line of wagons pulled by oxen, mules, or horses that was used to transport people and goods across the country. (p. 149)

waste (wāst) Materials that are no longer useful and are thrown away. (p. 205)

wilderness (wĭl´dər-nĭs) Land that has not been changed by people or their actions. (p. 122)

INDEX

Italicized numbers refer to pages on which illustrations appear.

Text *(continued from page iv)*

96–97 Reprinted with permission of Charles Scribner's Sons, an imprint of Macmillan Publishing Company from *The Desert Is Theirs* by Byrd Baylor, illustrated by Peter Parnall. Text copyright © 1975 Byrd Baylor. Illustrations copyright © 1975 Peter Parnall. **98** untitled Navajo poem, Copyright © 1978 by Richard Erdoes. Reprinted by permission of Sterling Publishing Co., Inc., 387 Park Ave. S., New York, NY 10016. **138–45 (xvi–xvii)** Chapters 1 and 2 from *Wagon Wheels* by Barbara Brenner, illustrated by Don Bolognese. Text Copyright © 1978 by Barbara Brenner. Illustrations Copyright © 1978 by Don Bolognese. Reprinted by permission of Harper & Row, Publishers, Inc. **154** "The Old Chisolm Trail", Copyright © 1939 by Kansas State Historical Society. Reprinted by permission of Kansas State Historical Society. **182** "Travel" by Edna St. Vincent Millay. From *Collected Poems*, Harper & Row. Copyright 1921, 1948 by Edna St. Vincent Millay. Reprinted by permission. **192–97** (text) *Once There Was a Tree* by Natalia Romanova, adapted by Anne Schwarz. Copyright © 1985 by K. Thienemanns Verlag, Stuttgart. English translation © 1985 by Dial Books for Young Readers. Reprinted by permission of the publisher, Dial Books for Young Readers. (illustrations) *Once There Was a Tree* by Natalia Romanova, adapted by Anne Schwarz, pictures by Gennady Spirin. Copyright © 1985 by K. Thienemanns Verlag, Stuttgart. Reproduced by permission of the publisher, Dial Books for Young Readers, and VAAP on behalf of the artist. **218** From "Johnny Appleseed" from *A Book of Americans*, Rosemary and Stephen Vincent Benet. Copyright 1933 by Rosemary & Stephen Vincent Benet. Copyright renewed © 1961 by Rosemary Carr Benet. Reprinted by permission of Brandt & Brandt Literary Agents, Inc. **246** Pronunciation key copyright © 1985 by Houghton Mifflin Company. Adapted and reprinted by permission from *The American Heritage Dictionary*, Second College Edition.

Illustrations

Literature border design by Peggy Skycraft.

Ligature 35, 37. **Brian Battles** 68, 69, 107. **Howard Berelson** 53, 74, 150, 222. **Chris Bjornberg, Photo Researchers** 2–3, 26, 42. **Jeanni Brunnick** 82, 83. **Randy Chewning** 45, 47, 119. **Susan David** 6, 22. **Roger Dondis** 105, 106(r). **Ebet Dudley** 48. **Randall Fleck** 70, 98, 106(l). **Mark Langeneckert** 32, 56, 85. **Joe LeMonnier** 5, 109. **Al Lorenz** 67, 124. **Laura Lydecker** 36. **Kathy Mitchell** 89, 101, 181. **James Needham** 29, 202. **Ed Parker** 9, 120, 126–127, 172, 225. **Judy Reed** 157. **Gary Toressi** 244, 245. **Cindy Wrobel** 186, 187, 191, 206–7, 210. **Oliver Yourke** 185. Other: **104** Source of painting: *Navajo Sandpainting Art* by Eugene Baatsoslanii Joe and Mark Bahti, Copyright © 1978, Treasure Chest Publications.

Maps

Ligature 59, 111, 165. **R. R. Donnelley & Sons Company Cartographic Services** Back Cover, 232–33, 234–35, 236–37, 238–39. **JAK Graphics** 19, 21, 35, 49, 52, 81, 100, 117, 122, 131, 135, 149, 156, 158, 159, 161, 171, 179, 199, 200.

Photographs

GH—Grant Heilman Photography; LC—Library of Congress; MA—Museum of the American Indian; NYPL—New York Public Library; PH—Photographic Resources; PR—Photo Researchers, Inc.; RBC—Royal British Columbia Museum, Victoria, BC, Canada; RR—Root Resources; SK—Stephen Kennedy; TBM—The Thomas Burke Memorial Washington State Museum; TIB—The Image Bank; TS—Tom Stack & Associates; TSW—TSW—Click/Chicago Ltd.

Front cover Peter Bosey, Missouri School for the Blind. **xviii–1** © David Muench. **2** © Jeff Apoian, Nawrocki Stock Photo (tl,br); © Geraldo Corsi, TS (c). **3** © Grant Heilman, GH. **4** SK (t,bl,br); © Lawrence Migdale, PR (b). **5** © Brian Parker, TS. **7** SK (t); © Four By Five, Inc. (l); © Eric Simmons, Stock Boston (cr). **8–9** SK. **18** © L. L. T. Rhodes, TSW (tr); © Frank Oberle, PH (c). **19** © Jim Appleyard. **20** © Fred McConnaughey, PR (tl); © Alain Thomas, PR (b). **20–21** SK. **21** Smithsonian Institution (tl); Dennis Hamm, National Park Service (br). **22** © Thomas G. Rampton, GH. **23** © Steve Proehl, TIB. **25** Thomas G. Rampton, GH (t); Steve Prochl, TIB. **26** © Ruth Dixon (tl); © Diana L. Stratton, TS (c). **26–27** © Grant Heilman, GH. **27** © Hugh Spencer, PR (tr); © Bob McKeever, TS (br). **28** © Steve Maslowski, PR (t); © Tom Mareschal, TIB (b). **30** SK (tl,tr,bl,br); © John Kaprielian, PR (tc). **31** SK (tl,cr); © Steve Maslowski, PR (tc); © Jeff Lapore, PR (c). **33** The Thomas Gilcrease Institute of American History and Art, Tulsa, OK (l); SK (r). **34** Grant Heilman, GH. **35** © Diana L. Stratton, TS. **36** SK; © Rod Planck, PR (l); © Leonard Lee Rue III, PR (r). **37** © Brian Parker, TS (l); © Larry P. Brock, TS (r). **38** SK. **39** SK. **42** © J. H. Robinson, PR (r); ©Joe McDonald, TS (b). **42–43** © Bob Firth. **43** © Kenneth W. Fink, RR. **44** © David Stoecklein, The Stock Market (tr); SK (r); © Don Murie, Meyers Photo-Art (b). **46** © Leonard Lee Rue III, TSW. **50** © Frank Oberle, PH (t); © Frank Siteman, PH (b). **51** © G. C. Kelley, PR. **52** © Grant Heilman, GH. **54** © Milton Rand, TS (t); © Stephen Krasemann, PR (b). **55** SK (tl); © John Cancalosi, TS (tr); © Bob McKeever, TS(b). **56–57** SK. **60–61** © Werner Forman Archive/Private Collection, NY. **62** © Chris Speedie, Image Finders (l); RBC (r). **62–63** Edward Curtis, LC. **63** © Eduardo Calderon, TBM. **64** RBC (l); Edward Curtis, University of Washington Libraries (detail) (r). **65** © Werner Forman Archive. **66** Eduardo Calderon, TBM (t); TBM (b). **71** LC (bl); © Dan Fivehouse, Image Finders (br). **72** TBM (bl); LC (br). **73** © Werner Forman Archive/Provincial Museum, Victoria, BC, Canada (t); H. I. Smith, American Museum of Natural History (b). **75** TBM. **78** © Brian Parker, TS (l); Philbrook Museum of Art, University of Tulsa Collection (r). **79** © Paul Conklin (t); Smithsonian Institution (b). **80** © Native American Images. **81** Museum of the Great Plains. **82** © Brian Parker, TS. **82–83** SK. **83** MA (c). **84** Smithsonian Institution. **86** Field Museum of Natural History. **87** USDA-NFS. **88** MA (l); Field Museum of Natural History (c). **90** Mesa Verde National Park (l); PR (b). **91** SK (r): NYPL; The Denver Art Museum; Peter Kaplan; Philadelphia Museum of Art; Georgia Historical Society; MA; Reader's Digest; SK (b): Holmes & Meier Publishers; MA. **94** © Mark Bahti (l); © Lois Moulton, TSW (c). **94–95** © Marcia Keegan. **95** Philbrook Art Center, Tulsa, OK (b). **98** © Craig Aurness, West Light. **99** SK (t,b); © Roger Wolken, TSW (cr). **102** Grant Heilman, GH. **103** © Terry Eiler, Stock Boston. **104** © Mark Bahti. **105** © Terry Eiler, Stock Boston. **107** SK. **112–13** Nebraska State Historical Society. **114** © UPI/ Bettman Newsphoto. **114–15** Malcolm Varon, Metropolitan Life. **115** © Jeff Apoian, PR (tr); New York State Historical Assn. (br). **116** NYPL (t); Plymouth, Pilgrim Society (b). **118** © UPI/Bettman Newsphoto. **121** SK. **123** © North Wind Picture Archives. **125** NYPL (t); The Farmer's Museum, NY (r). **126** SK. **128** SK, St. Louis Public Library (l); Missouri Historical Society (b). **129** SK, Jane Knirr Archive. **132** © Esto Photographics (l); Private Collection (c); **132–33** The Kansas State Historical Society, Topeka; © Time-Life, Henry Beville, Anne and Madison Grant. **134** © David Muench. **135** © David Muench. **136** © William Strode. **137** Joshua Shaw, Museum of Science and Industry, Chicago. **146** © L. E. Schaefer, RR. **147** The Granger Collection. **148** Elmer Fryer, Kathy Spangler Archive. **151** Denver Public Library (t); from *The Old West: The Pioneers*, Harald Sund © 1974 Time-Life Books, Inc. (b). **152** USDA (t); © Mary Root, RR. **153** National Archives. **154** © William Loren Katz Collection. **155** NYPL. **160** © North Wind Picture Archives. **161** LC. **162** Yale University Art Gallery (t); W. H. Jackson, Culver Pictures, Inc. (b). **163** © Jack Parsons, The Stock Broker. **166–67** © 1987 Kinuko Y. Craft. **168** © Tony Schanuel, PH (l); Greater Pittsburgh Office of Promotion (r); **168–69** © Grant Heilman, GH. **169** © John Livzey. **170** SK(t,l); © GH (b); **173** SK (t); © Grant Heilman, GH (b). **174** © Lee Balterman, Gartman Agency. **174–75** SK. **175** © William J. Kennedy, TIB (t); © Hans Wendler, TIB (c); © Michael Melford, TIB (b). **176** © Simon Wilkinson, TIB. **178** © Collection of the Equitable Life Assurance Society of the United States. **180** © Detroit Publishing Co., LC. (tr); © Robert Colton, Black Star (bl). **182** © Bob Taylor, FPG International. **183** Coverdale & Colpitts (tl); LC (br). **184** © Dave Gleiter, FPG International. **185** SK(t); © Tom Tracy, FPG International (br). **186** © Chuck O'Rear, West Light. **190** © Dennis Stock, Magnum Photos (l); © Alvis Upitis, TIB (c); **190–91** USDA-NPS. **198** D. L. Kernodle for FSA, LC. **200** © Spencer Swanger, TS. **201** © John Buitenkant, PR (t); © Greg Vaughn, TS (b). **203** USDA-FS Bauermeister (l); USDA-FS Frank Erickson (r). **204** © Mike Mathers, Black Star. **205** © Mike Andrews, Animals, Animals/Earth Scenes (l); © Roger J. Cheng (tr). **208** © Dennis Capolongo, Black Star. **209** Rick Benkof. **211** SK. **212** SK. **213** © John Fong. **215** SK. **216** © Brent Jones. **216–17** © Raphael Macia, PR (b); © John G. Herron, Stock Boston (t); © Grant Spencer, PR. **218** SK. **219** John Chapman, The Granger Collection (tl); SK (tr); © John Lei, Stock Boston (b). **220** Grant Wood, © Associated American Artists, NY. **223** © COMSTOCK. **226** © Minardi, Uniphoto Picture Agency. **227** © T. Kitchin, TS (t); SK, U. S. Postal Service (cl); © Pentagram (br); **227–28** SK, U. S. Postal Service. **230** Grantwood, © Associated American Artists, NY.

Picture research assistance by Carousel Research, Inc. and Meyers Photo-Art.